William Macneile Dixon

English Poetry from Blake to Browning

William Macneile Dixon

English Poetry from Blake to Browning

ISBN/EAN: 9783743329782

Manufactured in Europe, USA, Canada, Australia, Japa

Cover: Foto ©ninafisch / pixelio.de

Manufactured and distributed by brebook publishing software
(www.brebook.com)

William Macneile Dixon

English Poetry from Blake to Browning

UNIVERSITY EXTENSION SERIES

EDITED BY J. E. SYMES, M.A.
Principal of University College, Nottingham.

ENGLISH POETRY
FROM BLAKE TO BROWNING

ENGLISH POETRY

FROM BLAKE TO BROWNING

BY

WILLIAM MACNEILE DIXON

LITT.D., A.M., LL.B.

Professor of the English Language and Literature
in Mason College, Birmingham.

AUTHOR OF " A PRIMER OF TENNYSON " ETC.

SECOND EDITION

METHUEN & CO.

36 ESSEX STREET, W.C.

LONDON

1896

CONTENTS

CHAPTER I.

ERRATA

Page 17, second line, for "express'd" read "depress'd."

,, 54, line 11, for "place" read "places."

,, 56, ., 18, ,, "or" ,, "nor."

,, 78, .. 26, omit "of."

,, 92, ,, 9, ,, "and."

,, 107, ,, 19, ,, "and."

,, 112, ,, 16, for "but which" read "but rather those which."

,, 201, 1774, omit "Berkeley's 'Siris.'"

,, 202, 1806, ,, "Goethe's 'Faust.'"

,, 202, 1808, insert ,,

A SKETCH OF ENGLISH POETRY
FROM BLAKE TO BROWNING

—o—

CHAPTER I

POETRY AND ITS RELATION TO LIFE

'POETRY and criticism being by no means the universal concern of the world, but only the affair of idle men who write in their closets, and of idle men who read there.' This is how Pope, writing in 1716, felt it to be with poetry and criticism, that they were exclusively the affair of a comparatively small class, the leisured and cultivated few. The feeling of to-day is substantially the same. Readers have greatly increased in numbers since Pope wrote, but they have not, in any large proportion, come to care for poetry and criticism; they leave these, together with many other things, out of view, making no secret of their preference for that ephemeral literature which is of interest to-day, and is consigned to oblivion to-morrow. While, then, the newspaper *is* a matter of universal concern, poetry, although of immeasurably older, not to say nobler, birth, has never become so, and the promise that it will ever become so is

A

slight. Why is this? It is in part because there has always been, and still is, a wide-spread misapprehension of the nature and the office of poetry, or, in other words, of what poetry really is, and of what it can do for us. The critics have never made these things clear, but have, for the most part, darkened counsel with words. They have been content to address a minority which, in moments of foolish pride, is sometimes spoken of as 'a certain acute and honourable minority.' Criticism seems to have strengthened rather than dispelled the impression that poetry is a something altogether without weight or substance, a texture of light and air, like rainbow or sunset, pleasant to look upon, but, like them, incapable of being brought into any definite or profitable relationship with life. By many people poetry is thought to differ from science in this, that while the latter deals with facts, the former is concerned with abstractions; that while science is clear knowledge available for life, poetry is vague fancy available for no end, except, it may be, to feed the dreams of the indolent. In a practical age some apology for poetry is looked for. It is asked, 'Of what advantage is the study of poetry?' or 'What is it?' 'Is it a true thing?' But when the misapprehension spoken of is removed, apology will be idle; when once it comes to be clearly seen what the best poetry really is, and what it can do for us, nothing more will be needed. It will not be at all necessary to speak rapturously about it, to exalt its claims upon men's attention, or to trumpet the advantages accompanying a study of it in response to the trumpets that sound loudly on behalf of science. Although the poets are their own best apologists, there is still room for criticism, a criticism which shall address itself to those who, for some reason or other, have never felt drawn to poetical writings, who speak of themselves as without a taste for poetry. Criticism addressed to this class would be invaluable, for many such persons as are here spoken of ask, in all sincerity, as they have a right to ask, wherein it will be to their advantage to give time and attention that have such serious and, we may almost say, inexorable demands made upon them, to give this time and attention to a study which seems to have no very definite issue. ‘All about and around us,’ said a recent writer, ‘a faith in poetry struggles to be extricated, but it is not extricated.’ And it is so. Among those who have made friends with the poets this faith, this confidence in poetry, is very marked. They are satisfied of its quite incalculable worth, conscious that nothing can take its place, and that it has a kind of magic virtue peculiar to itself; but with the vast majority of readers, ‘a faith in poetry struggles to be extricated, but it is not extricated.’ Lovers of poetry, indeed, wish that it were otherwise, and are willing to give their testimony in behalf of what they love ; but while the minds of almost all men are so determinedly employed in other and far different directions, and, amid the tumult of voices proclaiming many gospels, to gain a hearing for the cause of poetry is not an easy matter. Poetry, we may safely say, will never attract the crowd, or draw to the seclusion of its shrine a multitude of devotees such as worship with passionate abandonment the great goddess Success, and so can never become, in any complete sense, a universal concern ; but we may indulge the hope that by means of a wise criticism the confines of the poetic realm will be indefinitely extended, and the benign influences of its sovereignty experienced by an ever-growing number of subjects. Plato, when he made his famous indictment against the poets, and shut against them the gates of his ideal commonwealth, did not pass a judgment from which there was to be no appeal. If good defence was made on her behalf, willing re-admittance was to be granted to Poetry ; she was to be allowed to return from exile. 'And to those of her defenders,' he said, 'who are lovers of poetry, yet not poets, I think that we may grant a further privilege—they shall be allowed to speak in prose on her behalf; let them show not only that she is pleasant but also useful to states and to human life, and we will gladly listen ; for if this can be proved we shall surely be the gainers, I mean if there is a use in poetry as well as a delight.' The task imposed upon the critics is the same to-day. Let them show that poetry is '*not only pleasant but also useful to states and to human life.*' Believers in poetry share with all men the desire to make the best of life, but ideas of what in reality are the best things in life, and where teaching in regard to them may be found, differ very widely. Confidence in poetry arises from the belief that into the poetry of the world have entered the opinions of the wisest minds of the world as to what these best things are, and that thus to become acquainted with poetry is to take a sure step towards wisdom. In the effort to frame for ourselves a just philosophy of life many of us have found the most reliable guides among the poets, and in their company have passed not only the most happy, but also the most helpful, hours of our lives. To show how it is that poetry has produced this faith in itself, to make the interest in it deeper, fuller, and more intelligent, is the first duty of criticism ; and an enquiry, however short and incomplete, into its nature, and the relation it bears to life, will therefore be serviceable as an introduction to the poetry of any particular era.

We may premise freely that a definition of poetry is impossible. Definition implies complete analysis, and in the end there always remains something in poetry that escapes analysis. And this is so, because poetry is rooted in and springs from the soil of human nature, and has to do with that nature in its relation to the world, and as it is constituted, with all its elemental powers and affections, with its primary facts. That nature, however far back we press the enquiry, can never be fully explained, and poetry also evades complete analysis. Not, indeed, that, strictly speaking, poetry itself is insusceptible of complete exposition, but rather the conditions of human nature, upon which its existence depends. Its genesis and nature are as inexplicable as that of life itself, for life throbs in it. Like all the other arts, it is wholly an achievment of man, of his creative instinct. 'The things which are said to be done by Nature, are indeed done by divine art,' and in the spirit of man has, from the first, been present a joy in creation, which we may suppose is akin to that felt by the Architect of the universe. Man's effort to express and to perpetuate his ideas through various mediums has resulted in the arts. Directed through the medium of colour it has produced painting; through the medium of sound, music; through the medium of language, poetry. But before poetry came to be a developed art, long before any conscious effort was involved in its production, the impulse in which its springs are set uttered itself at sight of the wonder and beauty of Nature in half-articulate cry perhaps, or, aroused by keen. joy or sorrow, in the spontaneous, vivid language of the feelings—an elemental or primitive song in the compass of a single gush of emotion.

Traced to its earliest beginnings, poetry is found associated with religious feeling. Into the dullest and least imaginative minds, content or forced to travel the monotonous round of experience prescribed by tradition and habit, come at times flying gleams from a larger world of ideas, a world which lies beyond the horizon of their daily lives. To that world poetry, like religion, is an avenue. It is a world of intenser emotional, intenser intellectual, intenser spiritual life than the one in which we hourly move. The impassioned language appropriate to these higher moods, elevated as much above ordinary language as the mood is elevated above ordinary moods, we speak of as poetical. When that language is metrically arranged, ordered or marshalled in a particular way, in a rhythmically effective way, we call it poetry.

In the childhood of races the only literature is poetical literature. Before the use of written symbols is known, while memory is the only library in which books can be stored, language, metrically ordered, is naturally, if not necessarily, resorted to as more easily borne in mind and less liable to undergo alteration in passing from mouth to mouth than language not so ordered. To the keeping of verse men entrusted their most cherished traditions, as well as their most sacred lore. Hence arose the idea that all poetry was inspired, that the poet was the speaker of divine oracles ; and thus from before the dawn of history poetry has been indissolubly associated with the highest instincts of the race, and has come to be a record of the profoundest convictions of men, their dearest hopes, their intensest griefs, and their most divine dreams. The river of poetry, as it flowed, parted into three main streams. Its earliest forms were, no doubt, hymnal, employed in worship. Then would come funeral and marriage hymns, songs celebrating victory or bemoaning defeat. Stories told in a kind of chanted verse

would very early be popular, and wandering minstrels, who
embodied in verse of their own manufacture tales of war,
love, or adventure, would be welcome guests in all primitive
societies.   The elaboration of such stories into a long con-
nected series, unified by their relation to one great hero or
one important event, would result in the epic or narrative
poem, such as the Iliad or Odyssey of Homer.   The word
epic, from its derivation (ἴπος, a word, a saying), denotes a
poem distinguished from a lyric in that it was without the
usual musical accompaniment, and was recited or chanted
rather than sung.   Thus, long before dramatic poetry came
to the birth, lyric poetry, expressive of pure emotion, and
narrative poetry, descriptive of persons, actions and events,
were familiar, and held in high estimation.   Poetry in
its earliest forms was religious; and an enquiry into the
origin of the drama discloses that this, an independent
branch of poetry, also sprang from religion, and was
originally, in its humble beginnings, part of the ritual of
worship.   The classic drama took its rise in the hymns
sung in honour of the God, at the festival of Dionysus ; the
romantic in the tableaux of scriptural scenes presented at
the Easter festival of the Christian Church.

In the opinion of Aristotle, poetry was a species of imitation.
But he so spoke of it, because, in his mind, poetry and the
Attic drama were almost interchangeable terms.   The whole
field of poetry was covered by Attic tragedy ; its lyric parts
were hardly less important than the speeches or dialogue by
which the action proceeded, and epic narrative had its
counterpart in the descriptive speeches of the messenger—
a character indispensable to the Greek stage, whence tradi-
tion and a severe taste had combined to exclude violent or
crowded spectacles.   Surveying the Greek drama, and find-

ing there an intermingling of lyric, epic and dramatic elements, Aristotle concluded that poetry was a species of imitation. And so in a sense it is; but as the mental horizon is pushed back, as the boundaries of knowledge are extended, the territories of poetry are widened. Pioneer poets explore the newly acquired lands of science or of philosophy, and the barren tracts, which at first promised nothing, are tilled, and made to bear poetic flower and fruit. Poetry does not deal with all the facts of which we may gain a knowledge. Piece after piece of knowledge is appropriated by the poet, and shown by him in its connexion with the moral, emotional or spiritual life; but in the outer intellectual court of our being must remain many facts which we acquire without emotion, and retain merely as conveniences. With general concepts rather than with particulars, and with such facts only as are susceptible of relation with the emotions, which connect themselves with the soul of man, can poetry deal. The condition of its existence is a vast and continually increasing body of such facts. We must never make the mistake that poetry is a chronicle of things instead of a chronicle of thought about things. When Wordsworth said, ' The poet thinks and feels in the spirit of human passions,' he meant that in the poet's mind thought was not disassociated from feeling—that his higher thoughts always tended to pass into the sphere of his feelings. And Tennyson has expressed the same idea when speaking of the poet. He said,—

' The viewless arrows of his thought were headed
And winged with flame.'

That is with the pure flame of emotion. Thus far regarding the material. But art, in which man imitates as far as in him

lies the example of Nature, 'art is the reason of the thing
without the matter.' What then of the art of poetry, the
essence of which is the moulding and fashioning of the
material according to the decree of the idea? The matter
of poetry is life, and thought about life ; its form is the way
in which that thought is presented. The material is partly
shared with the other arts and philosophies which are also
concerned with life and thought about life ; its form, its
manner of presentation of that material, is all its own. The
form that we recognise as belonging exclusively to poetry is
measured language, language dignified or beautified by the
marshalling of its component words in a certain order.
Beside the early mnemonic use of verse—to make poetry
a memorable thing, there is another quality which is of its
very essence. Constituted as we are, our sense of time,
harmony and proportion takes pleasure in the ordering of
words which constitutes the rhythmical beat of verse.
But this is not all. Rhythm is not merely a pleasurable
adjunct to poetry, it is, for a deeper reason, a vital part of
its being. The facts of life, as subjects of man's thought,
may find adequate expression in the words of prose, but
when thought is quickened by contact with love, wonder,
joy, indignation, grief, the words through which it is uttered
spontaneously tend to assume rhythmic form—impassioned .
thought runs to music. Upon this point stress must here be
laid, because rhythm, usually regarded as an ornamental
setting of the thought, ought rather to be taken as a clue to
the emotional state of the poet's mind. *Rhythm represents
emotion, and it gives rise to emotion ;* 'metre begins with
pulse-beat.' In the presentation of the facts which have
penetrated to the inner sphere of being, where thought and
feeling tend to become one, facts ennobled to the rank of

moral or spiritual truths, the deeper emotions of the poet are stirred, and by the vibration, the rhythmic movement of his verse, these emotions are represented and symbolised. The rhythm of the poem is the outward and visible sign and the correlative of the emotion that accompanied the thought in the poet's mind, and into it he translates not the idea alone but the intensity with which he feels it. Thus it is seen how rhythm communicates excitement similar to though weaker than that which gave it birth, and thus also it is seen that metrical arrangement which is without warrant in the feelings results in doggerel. Shakespere in his play of Julius Cæsar, desiring to convey the idea that the speech of Brutus over the body of Cæsar was a dispassionate logical appeal to the intelligence of the crowd, made by one who himself was far from anxious to arouse the emotions of his listeners, withholds from that speech all rhythmic life, reserving for Antony's address, wherein the orator makes a deliberate effort to kindle their passion by every rhetorical artifice, the metrical movement representative of his strong though restrained feeling. The complexity of structure or greater rapidity of lyric poetry typifies the high tension of the feelings, and, as the pulse responds to emotion, is quickened and intensified by it, so is it with the rhythm; in longer poems a simpler and less exciting movement is suitable, since the more intense the emotion the shorter will be its duration, and very complex rhythms cease after a time to produce their first effects, and are moreover difficult to sustain.

The exciting cause or motive cannot sustain the inspired or uplifted mood through long flights, and in such poems as 'Paradise Lost' there are stretches of table-land, with here and there an elevated plateau, while at times a great peak springs into the air to commune with the sun and stars. The rhythmic movement in such poems ought to be simple, yet sufficient to keep alive, during the comparatively low-lying passages, the idea of a general inspiring motive of which it is symbolic.   Essential poetry, however, throughout no long poem can be.

One frequently reads and hears it said that the end of poetry is to give pleasure.   It has other and higher ends; but a pleasure is none the less to be derived from it;—a pleasure in the form, whether from its fitness to the subject or its innate dignity and loveliness, a delight which is partly one of sense of the ear; and a pleasure in the apprehension of the force or beauty of the matter, of the thought which is its substance.   The object of the student will be to fit himself for participation in both these pleasures by an education of feeling as well as of intellect.

Discussing the relation of form and matter, Aristotle speaks of existence, the totality of existing things, as lying between the two poles of an absolutely formless matter and an absolutely matterless form; and we may think of poetry, or rather the sphere of poetry, as lying between the poles of prose and of music.   Prose depends for its value upon its substance, upon the weight of its thought rather than upon the setting of that thought, because it is in the main a vehicle for the conveyance of direct facts and direct thought about those facts.   With music it is different, since music is dependent for its value upon its form, form and matter being in music completely fused; in a word, the form of music *is* its substance.   The power of prose lies in the quality of its matter, the power of music in the quality of its form.   But that poetry is the highest, the most perfect, where it is impossible to determine with any kind of precision whether the charm, the power it wields, is resident in the thought or in its expression ; it is thought and language inseparably at one. The moment it becomes possible to say, ' Here the delight given is intellectual and due to the idea,' or, ' Here the delight given is sensuous and due to the form,' at that moment the poetry ceases to be of the highest quality. Poetry occupies the whole mid-region between prose and music, dealing with every fact of life which interests man as a sentient and intellectual being and may be imaginatively seized, and with every ideal which is susceptible of articulate expression. Whoever speaks of poetry as attaining supreme excellence by its style, the perfection of its form alone ; or whoever speaks of it as attaining supreme excellence by its substance, its thought alone, has not yet grasped the true nature of poetry. Perfection of form, subtle propriety of phrase will give to any poem grace, but not the higher merit of dignity ; depth or range of thought will secure for it value, but dignity which speaks the balance, which consists in intrinsic value of substance joined to intrinsic beauty of form, may still be wanting to it. So close and vital in the best poetry is the bond between the idea and the language that they are remembered together, for the art of the poet has pronounced a decree of indissoluble union between them. Lying, then, between the poles of prose and of music, poetry has a tendency to fall away into weakness towards the one or the other. It may become weak by inclining towards the sphere of prose, the sphere of logical statement, as in the case of Pope's poetry ; or it may fall from its high estate by invading the sphere or music, the sphere o. symbol and sound, as with Mr Swinburne. Our own century best exhibits the change between the poetry approximating to music inaugurated by Shelley and the poetry approximating to impassioned or philosophical prose inaugurated by Wordsworth and Browning. Music is, in a sense, inarticulate poetry; it gives expression to emotions which have not risen above the surface so far as to become ideas, or to be associated with definite thought. Upon the hidden strings of man's emotional nature music plays as the wind upon the Æolian harp. But in addition to his sentient, man has an intellectual life. Homer, by his 'articulately-speaking men,' meant men who had risen to the high dignity of thoughtful speech, to the use of words or language definitely expressive of ideas. Poems, whose strength lies in their colour or rhythm, almost imperceptibly approach and shade off into the sphere of music; they are music very imperfectly articulated. Why, some may ask, cannot poetry depend upon its rhythmic life alone? The music of words has indeed a delicacy, a melodious accent not to be matched by the keys of any instrument, because from its connexion with life each word bears with it a hundred whispers from the forgotten past; yet because words cannot form any but a single series of notes, a simple melody, because the harmonic, contrapuntal and orchestral effects of music are impossible to it, poetry cannot compete with music in the medium of sounds. Without a nerve of thought, it has no real or enduring vitality; but when so quickened, the lesson of the inner music is a higher one than that of the outer, the rhythm of thought is more thrilling than that of sound. 'It is not metres but a metre-making argument that makes a poem; a thought so passionate and alive, that, like the spirit of a plant or animal, it has an architecture of its own, and adorns nature with a new thing.' *

Aristotle, in the exposition of his doctrine of the 'Four

* Emerson.

Causes,' as it is called, tells us, that in order to arrive at a clear understanding of any individual thing, we must make four enquiries respecting it. We must ask what is the material which conditions its existence? What is its essential form? Through what agency is it produced? and What is the end attained by it?

If we examine the idea of poetry in this way, as indeed we have to some extent already done, we shall at once be satisfied that its existence is dependent upon the thoughts and feelings with which man views the world of which he is a part, and upon the actions and events of which he is a doer or a sufferer. That poetry has promise of being the strongest and most enduring that works upon the largest body of material, takes fullest account of the thoughts, the feelings, the doings and sufferings of the human race. To dramatic poetry, therefore, has been conceded the highest place, because its range is widest, because it addresses itself not to a representation of one phase of thought or of feeling, but to a representation of life in all its more striking phases, of life as it really is, and as it interests us. The high-water mark of its intellectual achievement is touched in a nation's dramatic poetry. In the epic there are elements which it has in common with drama and lyric, modified indeed, but present. The distinctive character of lyric poetry is its absolute subjectivity. Expressive of an individual mood, occasioned perhaps by some external circumstance, but, nevertheless, taking its essential colour and shape from the individual mind, lyric poetry is subjective. But it is something more. Wordsworth, in his ' Excursion,' is largely a subjective poet, but ' The Excursion ' is no lyric. The lyric is concerned with one memorable incident, one strong emotion, one imperative thought.   It is essentially a song capable of being sung by one voice or by a chorus, accompanied by some musical instrument.   And 'capable of being sung,' not that it must be sung to be rightly appreciated, but that it ought to have the qualities of song.   Lyrics have been regarded by some as the only true poetry, and such persons have declined to give the name to long philosophical or descriptive poems.   This judgment is unwarrantably narrow.   Dante Gabriel Rossetti is reported to have said that he hated long poems.   But he did not in reality hate long poems.   Nothing would have given him greater delight than a long poem, had it been possible to keep throughout the level of essential poetry. But it is not possible ; and so it comes that the lyric, which, in the hands of a master, may be from first to last at the same level, intense, flawless and complete, is the most fascinating of all forms of poems.   The lyric goes straight to the heart, for it is the song of the heart, and gives voice to the feelings that have their home in the secret depths of our being, to the affections that are primal.   Hence there is a closer similarity between the lyric poetry of all races than exists between any other of their art products.   In the expression of the deepest human feeling all nations tend to become one nation, all peoples to merge into one people. When we get down to the foundations we find the whole world kin.   Religion, affection, patriotism ; these are the chief springs of song ; or, as we may more at length express it, in our relation to the unseen world, and to the Supreme Power, ' in Whom we live and move and have our being,' in our relation to our fellows, and in our relation to the country of our ancestors, to which we are bound by indissoluble and sacred links ; in these relationships, whence spring the intensest and most spontaneous of our joys and sorrows, the roots of lyric poetry are deeply struck. Not definitely marked off from other poetry by versification peculiar to itself, lyric is distinguished by the quicker movement, the more vehement and emphatic form which will naturally arise out of and represent fervent passion, and divide off this kind of verse from the slower, statelier, graver movement proper to drama or epic.

'Poetry,' said Wordsworth, 'is the breath and finer spirit of all knowledge, it is the impassioned expression which is on the face of all science.'

In the nature of things, therefore, its foundations are laid ; and as man's knowledge of the true nature of things widens and deepens, and as that knowledge is brought into relation with human nature, additions are made to the materials of poetry, which concerns itself with truth and beauty that are enduring. Poetic material can never become exhausted.   The moods of races, like those of individuals, vary, and in each mood a new aspect of life is predominant or becomes emphasised by a temporary eclipse or suppression of others.   The poetry which appealed to the imagination in the Elizabethan epoch, poetry with a tone like Marlowe's

> ' Was this the face that launched a thousand ships,
> And burnt the topless towers of Ilium ? '

gave place to the poetry which appealed to the intelligence in the age of Anne, with a tone like Pope's,—

> ' 'Tis not a lip or eye we beauty call,
> But the joint force and full result of all.'

In its turn the poetry of manners gave place to that of romance, and in place of

‘ This mournful truth is everywhere confess’d,
Slow rises worth by poverty express’d,’

we have

‘She's o’er the Border, and awa
Wi’ Jock o’ Hazeldean.’

Nor can style and manner ever grow old; new modes of thought bring with them new and appropriate modes of expression. As no two faces are ever alike, as no two voices have the same tone, so in no two poets is the same accent discoverable. We need have no fear that as civilisation advances poetry will decay, as we are sometimes told; it will always be kept alive, in the words of Arnold, ‘ by the instinct of self-preservation in humanity.’

When we have investigated the *a priori* conditions for the existence of poetry, and found them to lie in the nature of things, in the world and man as a thinking sentient being related to the world, and when we have investigated its essential and distinguishing form, and found it to consist in language to which rhythm and movement have been communicated, ‘ the best words in the best order,’ a part of the inquiry still remains to be pursued. It is still left for us to ask by what agency does this impassioned expression of man’s thought about himself and the world come into being, and what end does it serve. Let us consider the answers to be returned to these questions.

And with respect to the first, we may say that it is through the agency of a particular type of mind. At all times, and among all races, the poet has been reverenced as a man divinely favoured, and not without cause. As we reflect again over the old conception of the poet’s character, that he was the bearer of divine messages to men, we see how natural it is, how real it

B

is. He is indeed a man favoured of heaven, for his thought comes nearer to intuition than that of other men, he feels more finely, more intensely, and more widely than they, and under the guidance of Nature herself, he speaks a purer and a more expressive language. 'The delight which a work of art affords seems to arise from our recognising in it the mind that formed nature again in active operation.' The poet, then, is a man quick to see and quick to feel, and when he presents in his poetry those aspects of truth or of beauty that have come home to him, he does so with entire conviction. For the moment, at least, he loses sight of himself, and feels himself the speaker of a disinterested word, a word to the whole human race. His message, dictated by no personal element, comes as an oracle from the central source of truth. Poets who excel in the mastery of the medium of words or language in which they work, are sometimes spoken of as the most consummate artists; others whose excellence lies in an intellectual mastery of life, in imaginative insight, in the discovery of new aspects of truth, with whose force or beauty our minds have not become familiarised, these poets are sometimes spoken of as *vates* or seers. We have seen, however, that before a man can claim the honourable title of poet, he must to some degree combine both powers, the power which consists in a mastery of the form, the medium of language in which he works, and the power which consists in an intellectual mastery of life, and in a kind of spiritual vision. Here, indeed, we are sailing perilously near the inhospitable shores of the land of metaphysic, which are full of terrible quicksands, and we might have endless riddles propounded to us in respect of this spiritual vision ascribed to poets, such as the formidable one for example,

How far is the human mind capable of acquiring a knowledge
of essential truth, of things as they really are ? We must
be content to waive such questions. They are of fascinat-
ing interest, but their discussion belongs to the sphere of
philosophy, and answers to them are fortunately not indis-
pensable, just as for the practical purposes of life they are
not indispensable.

We shall gain more that nearly concerns us by seeking
to find how best the last question propounded by Aristotle
may be answered. What is the end attained by poetry,
or what are its offices ? ' Let the defenders of poetry
show' (to revert to Plato's saying) 'not only that she is
pleasant, but also useful to states and to human life, and
we will gladly listen, for if this can be proved we shall
surely be the gainers—I mean if there is a use in poetry as
well as a delight.' We might fairly begin by saying that
there is nothing more useful than delight itself, wholesome
delight, that is, and that there is a profound educative
influence in it. This will be granted by all who have
mature knowledge of human nature and of life. And surely
if we are really anxious to preserve poetry as an unassailable
thing, we must be prepared to give up any of it that
ministers to emotional pleasure alone, without conducting
the emotions that it excites into healthy channels, that does
not, in the words of the great critic of antiquity already
quoted, 'purify or refine the passions' which it raises. To
stimulate the feelings with no further or nobler object than
the pleasure arising from stimulation, is enervating and
degrading. The honourable aim of poetry is the refinement
and purification of the native passions of the soul, and the
bringing of them into harmony with the divine reason. We
must then be prepared to give up all poetry which leaves

the intellect and the will out of account, and addresses man as if he were of emotion all compact. We must be prepared to retain only that poetry which is conducive to the health of the soul, '*rhythms that are the expressions of a courageous and harmonious life.*' *   There are certain powers belonging to man which he recognises as higher than others, of nobler lineage, as Milton says,—

> '—In the soul
> Are many lesser faculties that serve
> Reason as chief.'

To live according to the dictates of this chief faculty, to take its part against the lower impulses, is, most of us are agreed, the most serious, for it is the only real business of life. And here poetry can help us—here it is of instant and enduring worth. True poetry does not set itself the impossible task of ennobling the lower faculties to the rank of the higher, or of elevating impulses that tend downwards.

The great poets, as Principal Shairp said, 'would not have been content with any result short of this—the assurance that their work would live to awaken those high sympathies in men, in the exercise of which they themselves found their best satisfaction, and which, they well knew, ennoble everyone who partakes of them.' And he goes on to say that 'poetry makes common cause with all high things—with right reason and true philosophy, with man's moral intuitions and his religious aspirations. It combines its influence with all those benign tendencies which are working in the world for the melioration of man and the manifestation of the kingdom of God.'

Here, then, will be a completely satisfactory answer to give to Plato, and one, we may well believe, that would

* Plato.

give him pause before excluding the poets from his Republic. For, if in dealing with the things that, by common consent, by the witness of the whole human race, are highest and noblest, if poetry makes the cause of these things its own, what more serious than that it should not be universally welcome? To treat it slightingly or with indifference will be to show little solicitude or regard for the best causes. Poetry may be said to be on the winning side, for we have great confidence in the eventual triumph of the best causes. And in the meantime, while the struggle between the powers of light and the powers of darkness is being waged, poetry is welcome, and more than welcome, as a source of the most indispensable, the most precious, inspiring, sustaining, and consoling influences that can touch mankind.

A great poet will be at once a man of wider and deeper experience, of finer susceptibility, and of riper wisdom than his fellows; and more than other men he will assist us in developing in ourselves a wider range of sympathy, a purer life of the feelings, and higher moods of thought. In poetry we draw upon the experience of the world to enrich our own. The world in which we ourselves daily live and move is but a small world, a very minute portion of the world of men and women in existence, and when we think of the generations that have come and gone, our own lives and actions become almost insignificant in comparison. But those who learnt the world before us have left us a memorial—their treasured wisdom of heart and mind and soul — enshrined for the most part in the works of the poets, who are the chief speakers of the race. To make acquaintance with these works is to profit by the thought-harvests of the world; to make, as nearly as possible, our own experience identical with the universal.

Besides the misapprehension regarding the nature and the value of poetry, there is another cause which militates, and must continue to militate, against its universal acceptance. Aristotle said, 'My books are published, and they are not published.' It is so with all great books. The thoughtless or insincere person cannot learn in the school of Shakespere, Wordsworth will not whisper to him of the revelation of Nature, nor Browning tutor him in the grammar of psychology. The great authors have published, and they have not published. When we see the truth of this, we mark that it is a warning and a stimulus. These noble friends of ours are intolerant of the vulgar and the shallow, but their conversation with those who love their company is the wittiest, the most invigorating, the most brilliantly suggestive, the most consummate we shall ever know.

'Literature,' it has been finely said, 'is more than interpretation of external nature and human life; it is a revelation of the widening possibilities of human life, of finer modes of feeling, dawning hopes, new horizons of thought, a broadening faith and unimagined ideals.' * But in effect literature, and poetry which is the highest department of literature, are engaged upon the interpretation of Nature and of man. What a vast work is undertaken here! What patience, what reverence, what perseverance, what insight, what rightness of heart, what clearness of brain, what powers of reflection and of imagination, what intellectual grip is required for the task! It is hopeless to expect that we shall easily become masters of all that is to be learnt from the interpreters. And they will be the first to tell us how little they themselves know.

* Professor Dowden.

A complete revelation or interpretation is impossible, they say; and this, indeed, we know of ourselves. But the seizure of each new truth makes easier the apprehension of another. There is nothing isolated or self-existent in the universe, nothing independent, nothing to be understood outside its relation to what remains. The poet, the philosopher, and the scientist are not engaged upon different tasks—they are brother labourers in the same field. Their parts indeed are different, all have not the same gifts; and to the poet it is given to be most highly favoured, for the facts which the scientist discovers the poet interprets, and with a certain inspired instinct reveals their beauty and harmony and their worth in the spiritual life.

'Poetry,' it has been said, 'sprang from ease, and was dedicated to pleasure.' Had it been so, the generations since Plato would have acquiesced in his decision regarding it, and poetry would now rank as least among the arts. But poetry sprang from the human soul and from man's desire to gain a true knowledge of the universe and his own place in it, and his relation to the Supreme Power behind all phenomena, and it was consecrated to the service of his higher nature. As we have seen, it lives and moves among, and makes common cause with all high things, with right reason and true philosophy, with man's moral intuitions and his religious aspirations. And without these things, of which poetry espouses the cause, what would human life conceivably be? We cannot part with so powerful and so noble an ally of our higher and better selves. The rhythms expressive of courageous and harmonious life must remain with us.

There is a warning necessary for those anxious to enter upon the study of literature, and it is this—one much needed in these days of unconsidered enthusiasms on the one hand, and contemptuous indifferentism on the other,—Do not suffer yourself to be led into a depreciation of the value of a study of poetry, because it does not at first sight seem to have that intimate and vital connexion with practical life which is claimed for modern science ; nor become, on the other hand, a disciple in a narrow school which speaks of its own literary shrine as that in which alone the worship of true genius is celebrated. You may take it without doubt that poetry, which has taught, cheered and supported so many men of varied temperament and character, cannot fail to be beneficial in its influences upon your own life and character, and that it is no true reverence for genius that confines itself in a narrow groove of unqualified panegyric for one master. Two things only are required of you, faith in the inestimable value of good literature, a faith soon to be transformed into certain knowledge, and catholicity of taste in the endeavour to appreciate it, which is a potent charm against the cant and bigotry of sects and schools.

What remains to be said ?   What but that if these views of what poetry really is and what it can do for us be true, we cannot too early address ourselves to making some acquaintance with it ; so that, as Plato says, ' When reason comes we shall recognise and salute her as a friend with whom our education has made us long familiar.' ' If, by means of words,' wrote the late Cardinal Newman, ' the secrets of the heart are brought to light, pain of soul is relieved, hidden grief is carried off, sympathy conveyed, counsel imparted, experience recorded, and wisdom perpetuated. If, by great authors, the many are drawn up into unity, national character is fixed, a people speaks, the past and the future, the east and the west are brought into communication with each other.   If such men are, in a word, the spokesmen and prophets of the human family, it will not answer to make light of literature, or to neglect its study ; rather we may be sure that, in proportion as we master it in whatever language, and imbibe its spirit, we shall ourselves become in our own measure the ministers of like benefits to others, be they many or few, be they in the obscurer or the more distinguished walks of life, who are united to us by social ties, and are within the sphere of our personal influence.'

Thus poetry is at once a storehouse of inspiring forces and of everlasting memories.   And more, the unbought joys of life unoffered in the world's markets, these, too, the poets give, and give gladly : freedom and the breath of life to minds cramped and confined in the prison of some uncongenial occupation ; gladness from a source free to all and inexhaustible as Nature's elements ; consolation in every hour of disappointment of which the world is so . generous a dispenser, and indifference to the blows of circumstance or the averted face of fortune.

CHAPTER II

AN ERA OF TRANSITION

Thomson—Gray—Collins—Blake—Cowper—Crabbe

THE advance of civilisation is like that of an incoming tide. Between the wave that reaches far up the strand and the wave that succeeds to reach still further, there is a lull, and partial recoil. The history of literature, too, is a chronicle of wave-periods and lull-periods. Movements of thought and of society are the strong spiritual winds and the deep currents of passion that stir the surface and impel the waves of the ocean of literature. The spirit and temper of an epoch are minutely betrayed in the poetry produced by it, for literature is in reality history written by historians who write of their own times. Yet it is not a record of events, events are usually of small significance in themselves, but of the manner in which events come about, a record of the mental, spiritual and moral life of the world. 'The power of English literature,' wrote Matthew Arnold, 'is in its poets.' It is a true word, and a torch to light us far on an enquiry into the character and genius of the nation. The English people, a mixed race, despite its turn for the practical life, and its splendid development of that turn and devotion to it as distinct from the turn leading to the field of abstract thought, has always kept a place in its heart for the message of the poet. It has not reverenced, as other peoples, the musician or the painter or the sculptor, but the poet has never failed to awaken the deeper affections of its nature. In no other of the fine arts, save poetry, can it claim to have the lead, to have given birth to originative or stimulating ideas, or to have shown any superiority in its workmanship, either of delicacy or compass; its achievement in poetry is unrivalled and unique. Our present business is a consideration of a single group of poets who have contributed to the greatness of England's intellectual honour; but to read a character aright we must know something of its lineage; to understand the prevailing mood of any period, we must trace it, as we would a stream, to its sources.

What first strikes upon the ear of a student of English literature, is the diversity of tone in the poetry of different epochs. He catches a new accent in each succeeding age. In Chaucer, it is the note of the emancipated imagination, which for long centuries had pined in the monastic cell, or languished in the stifling air of narrow creeds. We catch the music of fresh delight in the outside world under the open heaven. When the busy lark, the messenger of day, salutes the grey morning in her song, it is—

' Farewell my book and my devocioun!'

The same note of the pure imagination, but the imagination become passionate, is heard in Marlowe :—

' Oh, thou art fairer than the evening air,
Clad in the beauty of a thousand stars !'

In Shakespere, it is the imaginative reason that is at work. When in the person of Macbeth he realises the profound world-weariness that overcomes even that stout soldier as he sees the high hopes of his ambition, for which he has renounced so much, fail him, it is not easy to miss the note of the imaginative reason :—

> ' To-morrow, and to-morrow, and to-morrow,
> Creeps in this petty pace from day to day
> To the last syllable of recorded time,
> And all our yesterdays have lighted fools
> The way to dusty death.'

Let us compare these familiar passages with others no less familiar to the readers of Dryden and Pope, and observe the new accent :—

> ' Stiff in opinions, always in the wrong,
> Was everything by starts, and nothing long.' . . .

> ' In squandering wealth was his peculiar art,
> Nothing went unrewarded, but desert.
> Beggared by fools, whom still he found too late,
> He had his jest and they had his estate ; '

or,

> ' Envy will merit as its shade pursue,
> But like a shadow prove the substance true.'

With Dryden and Pope it is no longer the emancipated imagination, or the impassioned imagination, or the imaginative reason; it is clearly the festival of the quick intelligence. In 'Absalom and Achitophel,' or 'The Essay on Criticism,' we recognise at a glance a brilliant expression of acknowledged truths, a clear, forcible rendering of definite organised chains of reasoning; in a word, reason presides over the mind of the authors. A bright, keen, intellectual seizure of the points of an argument, or the salient and telling features of a character or of an object— these give the piquant flavour to the verse of Pope and Dryden. We feel, as we read, that the minds which appear in it are alert and alive in a very marked degree, ready, as a clever debater is, to seize instantaneously upon a weak point in an opponent's argument, to discover the joint in the harness, and equally ready and capable of pressing home against it every point of his own argument, with an emphasis derived from arrangement and precision, and all the penetrative force of wit and epigram. As individual minds differ, so do races differ; and so does each race differ from itself at different stages of its history. During the fervid Elizabethan period, with its enthusiastic delight in human nature, and the pursuits and ambitions of men, little attention was bestowed on style for its own sake. The dramatists wrote straight out of the rich stores of their observation, and Nature guided their hands, making unnecessary the studied arrangement and careful polish, the graces of style indispensable to a literature whose subject-matter lacks vital interest, and needs to be made attractive and enhanced in value by a critical art. No one who compares the subjects of Elizabethan poetry with those of Restoration times can miss the essential difference there exhibited. In Shakespere's day the nation thought and moved as one man; it was aroused by the same interests, undivided allegiance was given by it to the same pursuits. But after the Civil War parties in religion, political parties and social distinctions drew sharp dividing lines among the people, throwing them into groups that thought and felt differently upon almost all important questions. The unity of the nation's life was broken in upon, and an age of controversy ensued. In such an age there is no space for the exercise of the imagination; it was imperative that the reign of reason should begin. The literature produced by such an age will inevitably be its mirror; it will be argumentative and didactic, possessed of the characteristics of a literature of debate, satirical, personal, direct. It will be occupied by questions of society or of the state rather than with the emotions or passions of individuals. Hamlet will be impossible for it, Lear will be out of place in it. We shall have rather many philosophical and scientific treatises, essays innumerable in prose and verse, and satires directed against public bodies and parties. Both subject-matter and style are revolutionised as we pass from the poetry of Elizabeth to that of Charles. The poet no longer writes out of his own observation and heart; he puts into carefully constructed verse a series of selected ideas upon any theme offered to him. He writes poems to order; he is no longer forced to write by the thoughts and emotions surging up in uncontrollable waves.

While Pope was still alive, James Thomson published his poem of 'The Seasons.' The possibilities of poetry in the school of the elder poet were exhausted. There was no more to be said about the subjects whence his inspiration was drawn, and they had never been sources of a very fervent inspiration. 'The fine madness which rightly should possess a poet's brain' was a tradition of the past. Pope drove a very docile pair of poetic steeds, and was so perfect an exponent of his art, that their management came dangerously near to being 'a mere mechanic art,' and to drive tolerably no very remarkable feat. 'I chose verse,' he tells us in his 'Design for an Essay on Man,' 'because I found I could express ideas more shortly than in prose itself.' Precisely. And the result proved the wisdom of his choice. Never were ideas more concisely or more pointedly expressed. But there are two things noticeable about them. First, they are common-place ideas, conventional, and such as, repre-

senting a class of society at a given period, do not appeal
to any other class; and, second, that, arising out of the
mind when unimpassioned, unwarmed by emotion, they
appeal only to the mind when unimpassioned, unwarmed
by emotion. They have their birth in the intellect, and do
not touch the heart. Pope's wit and flexibility of intelli-
gence keep his poetry alive; but when persons who did not
possess these qualities came to write in his style, although
they had acquired his trick of versification, they were unable
to do anything more than echo what he had already done.
Pope's poetry written by inferior hands failed to afford a
new kind of pleasure; and every poet who aspires to be
read must impart to his verse the power of giving a new
kind of pleasure. The name of every poet who retains his
place in the temple of fame suggests distinctive attributes;
it cannot be included among those of the select company
whose names are already there, unless he have added some-
thing all his own, different from the addition made by any
other, to the common treasury of song.

The poetry of the early part of the eighteenth century failed
to stimulate the generation that came after Pope; the ima-
ginative minds of the later half of the century found no
nourishment in it, and gradually they began to fall back on
earlier poets for the necessary stimulus—on Chaucer and
Shakespere and Spenser. Long before any new poetic im-
pulse arose powerful enough to support the poet at a high level,
a kind of borrowed or reflected light from the early natural-
ism of Chaucer and his successors gave some help to those
who looked for stronger guidance than that of Pope and
Dryden. The return of poetry to the natural emotions, to
universal feelings, to the permanent elements of human
nature as opposed to transient fashions and manners, was

gradual. Before the morning star of a new day of song appeared in the person of Robert Burns, a kind of poetry of the gradually brightening twilight, whose light of inspiration was, in part, at least, borrowed, and which yet possesses a beauty and a softness of colour which are its own, this poetry of the twilight fills the space between day and day. A revolution of some kind, new lights upon life, some exciting cause, fresh and originating and powerful ideas were needed to infuse the vital spirit into the dead frigid artificiality in which the classic tendency had become exhausted. Writing about thirty-five years after the death of Pope, William Blake, the artist-poet, laments in a poem to the Muses that they had forsaken poetry.

'Whether on Ida's shady brow,
Or in the chambers of the east,
The chambers of the sun that now
From ancient melody have ceased ;

Whether in heaven ye wander fair,
Or the green corners of the earth,
Or the blue region of the air,
Where the melodious winds have birth ;

Whether on crystal rocks ye rove,
Beneath the bosom of the sea,
Wandering in many a coral grove,
Fair Nine, forsaking poetry !

How have you left the ancient love
That bards of old enjoyed in you !
The languid strings do scarcely move,
The sound is forced, the notes are few !'

This was written in the lifetime of Dr Johnson, about the time that Cowper was publishing his poem of the 'Task, and long after the deaths of Thomson and Gray. Blake's position is that of a herald of the poetic glories of the dawn of the present century. He was, though born many years before them, a kinsman of Wordsworth and of Coleridge; and his aloofness from his own age, his intellectual independence mark him out as a conspicuous figure. But, although poetry had languished, the decay was due to the absence of arousing and stimulating impulses rather than to the dearth of poetic minds.

Gray and Thomson, Collins and Goldsmith, were all poets born, endowed in a very special sense with the true poetic nature, responsive to the subtle influences upon which it is nourished. The want of spiritual intensity in the times was blighting to poetry. Take up Thomson, the earliest of this group of poets. He felt keenly the disease, and ascribed it to the artificial life of cities with their crowded *salons*, their fashionable inanities, and their ignoble ambitions. For him the only remedy seemed to be in retirement to a country life amid country sights and sounds. So he turned for health of mind to the green fields and the long brown furrows of the tilled glebe, to the interchange of sunshine and shower, of Spring and Summer, and Autumn and Winter, to the wide open spaces that are untroubled by bustle and invaded by no foolish crowds. Though a love of Nature had from the first been present in Scotch poetry, due to a Celtic element, Thomson was the first writer to celebrate Nature for her own sake, to dwell lovingly upon her changing moods in their unchanging loveliness, and for this he must keep his place among English poets. Unfortunate in the time of his birth, his poetic instinct and power were sufficient to overcome, partially at least, the paralysing influences around him; and a passage such as this, descriptive

C

of the vast multitudes of sea birds on the western coast
of Scotland, is proof that he had indeed freed himself from
the bondage of the school of Pope—

> 'Where the northern ocean in vast whirls
> Boils round the naked melancholy isles
> Of farthest Thule, and the Atlantic surge
> Pours in among the stormy Hebrides ;
> Who can recount what transmigrations there
> Are annual made ? What nations come and go ?
> And how the living clouds on clouds arise ?
> Infinite wings ! till all the plume-dark air
> And rude resounding shore are one wild cry.'

The Elizabethan poets had almost exclusively treated of
man, his actions, passions and thoughts ; and, indeed, the
thoughts, passions and actions of men must for ever remain
as the supreme subject for poetry.   But none the less in the
beauties and teachings of Nature may the poets be versed,
for man is the child of Nature, cradled in her embrace, fed
by her bounty, covered by her kindly dust in the grave.
This is a true view of Nature, but there is a view of
higher truth.   As the scene of the great passion-play of
human life, Nature draws to herself a meaning and a mystery
not altogether her own, but borrowed from a sojourn of the
deathless spirit of man in her realm.   And this is the view
of the greatest poets.

Besides Thomson, before Blake and Cowper, two men
lived and wrote who carried the art of versification, the pure
form of poetry to a highly-wrought perfection in a new
direction.   Collins and Gray, born within a year or two of
each other, though poets of a different order from each
other, were scholars who introduced into their own language,
as far as was possible, the classical metres and methods.

Neither of them wrote much. A very tiny volume would contain their collected works, but every line is chiselled to a degree of perfection never before seen in English poetry. It cannot be denied that the poems of Collins and of Gray are artifical, artificiality of style was inevitable; but they are in that highest style of the artificial where the art is so cunning that it conceals the art. They cultivated a very narrow strip of ground, but they made it a garden in which the flowers, if few, are of rare growth and delicate colouring.

Blake, as we have seen, longed for a return of the simplicity and passion of the Elizabethan time, and he stands a lonely precursor of the poetry that was to revive these qualities. He was not a child of his own age, but of that which followed his own, and which he lived to see. The 'Songs of Innocence and Experience' are full of the same sympathies that give the distinctive tone to the poetry of Wordsworth and of Coleridge—unalloyed delight in the simplest sights and sounds of Nature, a tender vein of feeling for childhood, and a passionate, disinterested fervour in the cause of the human race. Blake's poems, indeed, combine in a wonderful degree the most characteristic features of both the later poets. From his simplicity there breathes a like spiritual power; there is present in his poems the mystic vision of Coleridge, with the gentle innocence of Wordsworth. His was not a balanced mind, but it was visited by rare gleams of a pure and intense light, and his devotion to the ideal forms of goodness, truth and beauty, was that of a child. His recognition of them was no less intuitive and childlike. No strain of philosophic reflection is to be heard in his best poetry; it has the careless charm of a bird's note, the spontaneous, unpremeditated flow of one of Jonson's or

Shakespere's songs.   Blake felt, unconsciously perhaps,
that it is not in the massing of details that the poet's ex-
clusive province lies, but that his aim is accomplished when
he leaves upon the reader's mind one pure, simple, affecting
outline, one undying image of perfect feature.   This he
accomplished in many of his poems, and though his place
in the history of English literature cannot, by reason of the
smallness of his poetical contribution, be a high one, it is
unassailable because of its rare quality, its sincerity of
motive, its purity of ideal, its unaffected graces of form, and
because he first sounded, in a degenerate age, the trump of
liberty.

'What Pope is to our fashionable and town life, Cowper is
to our domestic and rural life. This is perhaps the reason why
he is so national.' * The choice of noble themes has always
been a chief care of most poets. Among the Greeks, the
subjects of the epic and the drama were drawn from the well-
known heroic tales of their ancestors, in the days when the
gods visited earth, and took part in the affairs of men. Virgil
and Dante chose large subjects, Shakespere treated of a
great historic cycle of events and persons, and Milton's
argument is the highest of all.   But while the subject may
elevate the poem, it is quite as likely that its weight may
prove too much for the adventurous author.   It needs the
shoulders of an Atlas to support the superincumbent world,
and not seldom has it happened that the very majesty of his
theme has been the cause of a poet's failure.   Keats knew
this when he abandoned his poem of 'Hyperion.'   Milton
began a poem on 'The Passion'; 'but finding it to be above
the years he had when he wrote it, and nothing satisfied

* Bagehot.

with what was begun, left it unfinished.'   On the other hand,
to treat of trivial or commonplace matters so as to make
them shine with an unexpected beauty, is no easy task.
Cowper has done this for us.   In the very names of his
poems he suggests the simplest and most domestic themes,
and the quiet stream of his verse flows by the path of daily
life, never turbid with passion or swollen with excitement,
but bright and limpid and sweet-sounding.

> ' Home-born happiness,
> Fireside enjoyments, intimate delights,
> And all the comforts that the lowly roof
> Of undisturbed retirement, and the hours
> Of long, uninterrupted evening know.'

Cowper, first of English poets, dared a consistent simplicity
of subject and of treatment.   He discerns with the poetic
eye the beauty of the most inconspicuous natural objects,
nor does his interest in them ever wane.   Out of the uncon-
sidered trifles, left by all the other poets, his poems are
woven, for he is a faithful student of the details of life.   As
he describes natural scenery, we seem to hear the voice of a
companion upon a country walk directing our attention to
the features of the scene :—

> ' Here the grey, smooth trunks
> Of ash, or lime, or beech, distinctly shine
> Within the twilight of their distant shades :
> There lost behind a rising ground, the wood
> Seems sunk, and shortened to its topmost boughs.
> No tree in all the grove but has its charms,
> Though each its hue peculiar ; paler some
> And of a warmish grey ; the willow such,
> And poplar that with silver lines his leaf, . . .

> The lime at dewy eve
> Diffusing odours ; nor unnoted pass
> The sycamore capricious in attire,
> Now green, now tawny, and ere Autumn yet
> Have changed the woods, in scarlet honours bright.'

It is not in all moods, we must confess it freely, that
Cowper can be approached with any prospect of enjoy-
ment.   The fault lies here, that, owing to the circumstances
of modern life, its rapidity and complexity, owing to the
presence all around us of sources of constant mental excite-
ment, we acquire what Wordsworth spoke of ' as a thirst
after outrageous stimulation.'   A distaste for literature which
affords no keen mental excitement is almost unavoidable,
and we cease to enjoy such quiet pleasure as is to be had
in the society of Cowper or even Wordsworth.   But if we
are at all concerned for the health of our minds, some effort
must be made to preserve a taste for the quieter walks of
literature, the simpler flavours, the less voluptuously-scented
flowers.   To maintain a due mental balance, a fresh interest
in all that enters the sphere of thought or action is essen-
tial ; for a loss of the power of feeling follows close upon a
neglect of the less exciting aspects of life, the fountains of
natural emotions are dried up, and ennui and pessimism
find ready entrance into the citadel of the heart.   The
poetry of Cowper, because it recalls us to simpler pleasures,
recalls us from the hurry and bustle of our complex attrac-
tions, from the false cosmopolitanism which threatens to
overwhelm all domestic interests.   The burden of the sor-
rows of the whole world is, now that the world has become
so small a place, laid upon every man.   But to live abroad
over all the earth, to make its innumerable problems ours,
is to take upon us more than we can bear.   To preserve
the balance is needful, and in the delight which Cowper

feels for the minor elements, a vital and necessary part of existence, there is assistance in maintaining this balance. 'When he is great,' says Mr Palgrave, 'it is with that elementary greatness which rests on the most universal human feelings.' When you come to think of it, this is true of all the best poets. When they are great, it is with that elementary greatness which rests on the most universal human feelings. Not by searching for unique experiences, by delineating an unusual mood of mind, by the invention of startling paradoxes, can a poet become the favourite of a nation; but only when his words spring from the experience he shares with the whole human race, when he speaks the language of the heart which no man fails to understand.

' Mortals speak many tongues, the immortals one.'

The whole effort of the poets of this transition period was towards naturalness; naturalness in thought and expression, in the room of ingenuity and artificiality. This conversion to naturalness in poetry was accompanied by its old passion for humanity, which had been lost in the conventionalism of the so-called Augustan age. But the new delight in humanity is more reflective than that of the school of Marlowe; there is less of passionate joy in it, but the place of passion is taken by a graver, we may even say a more spiritual mood. Its sign is a certain tenderness, a sympathy for the meaner aspects of man, his weaknesses and failures, which is lacking in Elizabeth's men. Marlowe and Ben Jonson would have been impatient of the feeble-minded or uncourageous person, their eyes were bent in admiration on the strong and the heroic and the successful. The sympathy with failure, so strongly marked in our developed moral sense, has small place, if we exclude Shakespere, with any poet before Cowper. The individual 'fashioned in all noble and gentle discipline' is not to be any longer the poet's ideal, his dream is of a perfected humanity. Mankind, toiling painfully up towards the light, the sin and error as well as the intellectual and spiritual achievement of the race, he takes all into one wide, comprehensive view. The man who will rejoice most truly over the victory is the man who has felt most keenly with the victor during the struggle, and while the issue was still a doubtful one. The attitude of the great poet is finely described by the late Dean Church in speaking of Dante :—

'Fresh from the thought of man's condition as a whole, fresh from the thought of his goodness, his greatness, his power, as well as of his evil, his mind is equally in tune when rejoicing over his restoration, as when contemplating the ruins of his fall. He never lets go the recollection that human life, if it grovels at one end in corruption and sin, and has to pass through the sweat and dust and disfigurement of earthly toil, has throughout compensations, remedies, functions, spheres innumerable of profitable activity, sources inexhaustible of delight and consolation, and at the other end a perfection that cannot be named.'

Like Wordsworth, Cowper was not a student of books, nor was he an eager reader of poetry other than his own, but Milton he knew well, and learned his blank verse from that great master of metrical harmonies. 'Why not try blank verse?' said Lady Austen to him; and in 'The Task' the fetters of the heroic couplet were thrown off, and an essential step taken towards the music and liberty of nineteenth century poetry. Poetry, as he himself tells us, was his amusement. 'Despair made amusement necessary, and I found poetry the most agreeable amusement ' but it was amusement to which he devoted his full mental strength, and the apparent ease, spontaneity and naturalness of his verse were the outcome of conscientious labour; it is nowhere marred by carelessness. Cowper and Crabbe are the English counterparts in poetry of the Dutch school of painters. Real as was Cowper's feeling for nature, faithful as are his transcripts of her varying moods or phases, he never dreamt of 'the consecration,' or 'the light that never was on sea or land'; that revelation, the apocalyptic vision, are Wordsworth's, and Wordsworth's alone.

Smooth lawns, the trim parterre of an ordered garden, Nature improved upon by man, are all that Pope gives us. Cowper is the poet of virgin woods, the hill and valleyland of English landscape, observantly accurate in his delineation of externals. But in Wordsworth, 'the sense of something far more deeply interfused' animates, transforms and transfigures, and we exchange the details of the phenomena presented to the eye and the mind for the vision that awakens and dilates the soul. Far more effectively was the revolt against conventionalism carried on by the calm persistence of Wordsworth and the fiery energies of Burns and Byron; but that revolt was initiated by Cowper—he was a good soldier in the van of the army of freedom. Wishing, above all things, to be a guide to a better life, he set himself to reclaim the age. He did not indeed reclaim the age, but he represents the beginnings of the forces that were destined to work for the renewal of Society that came later. He marks the epoch which, ceasing to pay exclusive regard to the political aspects of things, began to look towards the social reforms which are the paramount concern of to-day His letters best tell his life. Southey thought him the greatest master in English of that lost art, letter-writing.

Taken in conjunction with 'The Task,' they give a full-length portrait of the artist painted by himself. To 'The Task' every reader must go whose feeling for Cowper is ever to become an affection. In it a gentleness and a *naïveté*, a sweetness and a melancholy, a tender grace and a subtle pathos, a quiet humour and a pure religion combine to produce a charm unmatched elsewhere. 'Our highest master in simple pathos,' Cowper's vein of humour, delicate, pointed, and yet utterly guileless, adds to its peculiar power. Humour like that of Cowper or of Lamb, emanating from a life of almost unbroken sadness, intensifies the pathos of the life itself. Perhaps, of all the forms of mental disease, the most appalling is religious insanity, and there is no sadder life among the poets on record than that of this gentle victim of a disordered imagination. In his poem of 'The Castaway,' describing the sailor who, falling from his vessel, perishes in mid-ocean, for a moment or two a lonely speck amid the foaming yeast of its waves, he passes from him to speak of his own fate as more terrible—

> ' No voice divine the storm allayed,
>   No light propitious shone,
> When snatch'd from all effectual aid,
>   We perished, each alone ;
> But I beneath a rougher sea,
> And whelm'd in deeper gulfs than he.'

To Edmund Burke is due the rescue of a poet from oblivion, perhaps from death by want, whose name is associated with Cowper's as standing midway between the school of Pope and the school of Wordsworth. Crabbe, the poet laureate of East Anglia, cannot be passed over in any sketch, however slight, of the period to which he belongs. ' Nature's sternest painter, yet the best,' was Byron's opinion of him, and, although fate will be against his acceptance by any large body of readers, those who can read him will always read with the respect due to strong and original genius. As portrait or as landscape painter he impresses equally; he never fails to leave an impression of power in the gloomy realism of his village tales. Poetry is here, for the first time, the vehicle of social reform.

The poets just mentioned were the forerunners of the revolution in its meridian splendour. If we take up Mr Palgrave's *Golden Treasury*, turn to the third book, and read there the first poem by the Scotch peasant, Robert Burns, we shall realise far more vividly the change which came over the spirit of English poetry than by reading a hundred critical histories. Or if we read the same untaught poet's 'Vision' of his own native land in its sad estate, we cannot but feel that here again, after a silence of more than a hundred years, the note of high poetic passion rings clear and true.

'As I stood by yon roofless tower,
   Where the wa'-flower scents the dewy air,
Where the owlet mourns in her ivy bower,
   And tells the midnight moon her care; . . .

By heedless chance I turned mine eyes,
   And, by the moonbeam, shook to see
A stern and stalwart ghaist arise,
   Attired as minstrels wont to be.

Had I a statue been o' stane,
   His darin' look had daunted me;
And on his bonnet graved was plain
   The sacred posy—" Libertie !"

And frae his harp sic strains did flow,
   Might roused the slumb'ring dead to hear;
But, oh ! it was a tale of woe
   As ever met a Briton's ear.'

With Burns we enter the field of what are called 'modern ideas.' In German philosophy the impetus was given to abstract thinking, an impetus which was conveyed beyond the borders of the country of Kant, and, passing into England, began to transform men's views of life. The strongholds of conventionality and tradition were stormed, a new spirit went forth, breaking up all the old moulds of thought, acting as a chemical solvent upon the crystallised, unexpansive ideas so long current, and setting up new combinations. 'Thus rises the modern man,' says Taine, 'impelled by two sentiments, one democratic, the other philosophic.' The current of democracy flowed from France, that of philosophy from Germany. Under the combined influences of these two forces, invigorating, electrifying the inanimate body, England put forth the powers so long lying dormant. Once more from the fields of literature, as in Shakespere's day, a free, fresh breeze strikes across our senses. Glints of Spring sunshine begin to play across the heavy atmosphere and the stagnation of Winter is at an end.

CHAPTER III

THE SPIRIT OF POETRY IN REVOLT

Burns—Byron—Elliott

THE eighteenth century was an age of <u>self-complacency</u>. It saw no pressing necessity for sweeping reforms, it discerned no place for the enthusiast in the cause of progress. 'Things are very well as they are,' it said; 'confusion and disorder follow in the track of enthusiasm, and of all evils, confusion and disorder are the worst.' Eighteenth-century philosophers were inclined to admit that there was a God, and another world than that of which our senses give evidence, but it was not a matter about which anyone need for the present greatly exercise himself. Time would tell, and meanwhile here were numerous objects of interest to make this world sufficing to all sensible men, who might be recognised by their reluctance to abandon it even in speculation. Eighteenth-century moralists were equally sober-minded; they made a sharp division between the spiritual and the material universe, and disliked above all things the Puritan habit of attaching spiritual significance to material actions and the terms which connoted them. 'Right' and 'Wrong' were terms of relative meaning, no eternal or essential division existed between the acts to which mankind habitually referred these designations, it was a legal

fiction to speak of any divine sanction behind them.   As
for religion, religion was indeed an excellent thing in its
way, in its own time and place, but like most things, as
the Puritan excesses proved, out of its own time and place,
it came near being intolerable.   Religion was one thing,
life was another thing; their spheres touched, but were -
not concentric.   A religion thus separated from life was
necessarily formal.   Without a vitalising spirit to mould it
from within, it was ruled by convention and tradition from
without; and as it was with religion so it was with all social
institutions, the formal man, not the natural man, was the
gentleman of the period.

Burns and Byron, peasant and peer, far removed from
each other in circumstances of life as well as of birth,
resemble each other in a striking particular, their attitude
towards Society was one of revolt.   Alike in this, their
treatment at its hands was not dissimilar.   They suffered
alternate praise and blame, extravagant and unmeaning.
Both sprang at one bound into the highest niche of the
temple of fame.   Both were fondled and courted for a
season, and in the end became exiles from the society
whose darlings they had been; and in the hearts and in
the poetry of both burned the ardour of indignation and
scorn.   Primarily intellectual as was the revolt in which
Burns, and afterwards Byron, played such conspicuous
parts, the passionate minds of these poets carried into the
zeal of revolution an element of strong personal feeling.
Thus far the likeness may be traced, but we must pause
to mark differences.   Burns preceded the French Revolu-
tion—Byron followed it.   Although the ideas which took
political shape in the proclamation and establishment of
the French Republic, the ideas which group themselves

round the central conception of the brotherhood of man, were in the air when Burns published his first volume of poems, they were ideas only. The excitement of their translation into practice was yet in the future. Byron, moreover, was from the first in the world's eye, Burns toiling with his hands and in provincial obscurity; and it is strange to note that while the natural ambition of the one was thwarted by the extreme of poverty, the other affected to despise the admiration his person and genius compelled. The stability of Burns' position as poet is secured by this, the unaffected truth, sincerity and natural-ness of his lyrical cry. Unfettered by rules of poetic procedure, his songs are the spontaneous gush of over-flowing emotion. The passion of love or pity or rapture gathers in his breast, gathers and rises until it is no longer controllable, and finds an outlet and relief in the vibrating music that pulsates in unison with the throbbing pulses of his heart and head. What is there in

> ' Had we never loved sae kindly,
> Had we never loved sae blindly,
> Never met, and never parted,
> We had ne'er been broken-hearted ; '

in

> ' Drumossie moor—Drumossie day—
> A waefu' day it was to me ! '

in

> ' I sigh'd and said amang them a'
> Ye are na Mary Morison ' ?

There is nothing save the direct, simple, affecting voice of human nature deeply stirred, as every heart has been stirred, by the events of life, which, however familiar, are

never old; by the feelings which, however fresh in indi-
vidual experience, living an immortal life as they do in
the world's memory, are never new.

Language is not chiselled and filed and polished here
to express subtle conceptions or carefully-chosen, appropri-
ate imagery; it is not rhetoric or rhymed ideas; it is the
language that Nature speaks—the language of truth and
passion.   Here it is scarcely legitimate to speak of the
poet's art, for he seems but a chosen mouth-piece for the
utterance of universal sentiment.   The songs of Burns
well up from the central springs of being, their beauty or
melody is not analysable.   We know that they formed in
his mind to the accompaniment of remembered music of
old and familiar airs, rose into perfect shape as when
Ilion to Apollo's lyre 'like a mist rose into towers.'
There is but one note which can without hesitation be
said to ring resonant and pure in the poetry of the Scotch
peasant, that heard in his songs.   It is the only faultless
part of his work, and in it he touches the highest limit;
his reach in lyric poetry was higher than any since Shake-
spere.   For some minds there will always remain the
accent of insincerity, a pathetic accent sadly ironical, in
his humour.   His humorous poems are no doubt the
work of a genius; but with very few exceptions, the more
outrageously merry they are, the more distinctly do they
give this impression of insincerity.   A somewhat inde-
finable suspicion is awakened by them that the very
wit and humour of the scenes he paints so graphically
are recognised by Burns as a hollow wit and a humour of
despair.   As has been the case with so many English
poets, his poetry is only a half-result, if indeed it be even
a half-result.   Born poor, he remained poor until the end.

'I had felt early,' he tells us, 'some stirrings of ambition, but they were the blind gropings of Homer's Cyclops round the walls of his cave. The only two openings by which I could enter the temple of fortune, were the gate of niggardly economy, or the path of little chicaning bargain-making. The first is so contracted an aperture I never could squeeze myself into it; the last I always hated, there was contamination in the very entrance.' The gates were barred against him, and the possibilities of a career, literary or social, for which his genius marked him out were irreducible to any trial. Although he lived in an era of dawning cosmopolitanism, and new horizons met the far-darting vision of his genius; although he has supreme right to the title of the first poet of democracy, of the creed that hopes to make true the prophecy,—

> ' That man to man, the world o'er,
> Shall brothers be for a' that.'

he is far from the attitude of Shelley, that flaming sword in the cause of revolution. Burns is a true revolutionary against the hollowness and affectations of his time both in poetry and life; but his strength is in his acquaintance with human affections, in tenderness of heart rather than in any iconoclastic fervour; in a word, he is strong as a poet, because every fibre of his being was athrill with inexhaustible sympathy. For the higher poetry—poetry not of passion merely, but which, treating of action and thought, demands structural talent, wide-extended knowledge, imaginative insight, for this poetry he was disqualified by the circumstances of his life as well as by the limitations of his mind. Carlyle believed Burns to have possessed mental force equal to all undertakings, but the evidence for such a conclusion is insufficient. He is pre-eminently the poet of passion. He sang of what all have felt, but his thought does not soar, nor do his *dramatis personæ* live and move. Under the gaze of Dante or of Shakespere, thought, passion, action, character, temperament, circumstance draw together, are taken in by the imagination as a whole, fall into their relations with each other, and in such art the elements of life and of nature are unified. These are not the poets of detail, of passion, or of introspection, or of circumstance; but of the round world, comprehensive of greatness and of littleness, of evil and of good, of love and of hate, of strength and of weakness, of will and of fate. Burns is a pure lyrist, his poems turn each on a single thought, his imagination has no powerful sweep of wing, the upper æther was not for him as it was for Milton, his own natural home; but he knew the secret chambers of the heart, the pathos of its unfulfilled dreams and its broken idols, and no less the joys of its moments of ineffable rapturous content.

England was rich in song-writers during the later part of the sixteenth and the early half of the seventeenth century, for she was rich in dramatists, few of whom were unpossessed of the lighter touch that carves the cameo of verse. The most exquisite little gems of lyric poetry are set in the pure gold of their stately dramatic measure. Take one snatch of Heywood's to illustrate the fresh heartiness of that open-hearted, great-minded, strong-handed age :—

> ' Agincourt, Agincourt, know ye not Agincourt?
> Where the English slew and hurt
>   All the French foemen?
> With our guns and bills brown,
> Oh, the French were beat down,
>   Morris pikes and bowmen ! '

The art of song-writing died in Restoration times. It was kept alive by the strong loyal emotions of the Cavaliers, and by the intense spiritual zeal of the Puritans during their memorable struggle, but it languished and utterly decayed with the conventional diction and forced graces of the school of Pope and Addison. Although unsupported genius may accomplish much, the highest intellectual reaches have been attained by men who stood upon foundations previously laid. Inherited wealth in good hands may become the nucleus of a princely fortune. Sophocles' perfect art was in large measure due to a careful study of Æschylus, Shakespere was not above profiting by the genius of Marlowe, Tennyson drew into his poetic net beauties from every great literature of the world. Just as Shakespere may be said to have climbed to supreme place among the dramatists upon the shoulders of his dramatic brethren who preceded him, Burns towers pre-eminent as the lyrist who was heir to all the best qualities of a nation's songs. Only when he abandoned the Scotch dialect was Burns artificial, when he wrote English the bondage of the classical school was upon him. His real progenitors were the ballad and song-writers and the rustic rhymers of his own country, to the poetry of English culture the debt he owed was trifling and of doubtful value. Scotch song-writers, whose name was legion, had covered the whole ground before the advent of their peasant successor, who was to become their prince, the lord of song by right and by acclaim. That he was heir and master of this demesne is small reason for asserting his title to sovereignty over the whole poetic realm had he chosen to enter into possession. Carlyle regretted that 'our son of thunder should have been constrained to pour all the lightning of his genius through the narrow cranny of Scottish song—the narrowest cranny ever vouchsafed to any son of thunder.' By an error of judgment of a like kind he regretted that Scott did not direct his powers towards some nobler end than the revival of the picturesque side of feudalism. That a man can do one thing transcendently well is small reason for supposing him capable of splendid achievement in a field foreign to that which he tills with unique success. The universal genius is a rare growth; Nature does not bestow all her favours upon one of her children, she is an impartial mother, and grants to each gifts differing in degree and in kind. To Burns she gave the 'great poetic heart,' to possess which is to be a child of sorrow as well as of joy, and a voice than which no sweeter ever broke silence; but she withheld from him that august and luminous mind in whose serene and contemplative depths all discords melt into harmony under the dominion of a reposeful, guiding will. To set the poetry of Burns beside the world-poetry of Sophocles, of Dante, or of Shakespere, or to speak of his intellectual depth and range as at all commensurable with that displayed in 'The Antigone,' 'The Divine Comedy,' or 'King Lear' is to betray incurable incapacity for the formation of sane or reliable judgment. Burns must stay with us and with the generations to come because of the essential poetry of such lines as these that recall the Elizabethan accent:—

> 'O, my love's like a red, red rose
> That's newly sprung in June;
> O, my love's like a melody
> That's sweetly played in tune';

or these, in whose pathos centres in briefest suggestion a tale as old as human nature:—

> ' Thou'll break my heart, thou bonnie bird,
>   That sings beside thy mate :
>   For sae I sat and sae I sang,
>   And wist na o' my fate.'

or these that in their very movement breathe defiance :—

> ' Sae rantingly, sae wantonly,
>   Sae dauntingly gaed he ;
>   He play'd a spring, and danc'd it round,
>   Below the gallows tree ' ;

These are verses of a writer who is safe beyond the reach of the tides of time that encroach upon so much fair territory, of a writer upon whom the envious years scatter no concealing dust.   In these there is no false pastoralism, no pseudo-sentiment, no choicely culled images, no trite wisdom, no inert philosophy.   They are appeals not to man as a member of a group of persons living under certain traditional habits and customs, calling themselves society, but to man as man.   Traditional habits and customs, fashionable views and sentiments, are unceasingly undergoing change, a wind passes over them and the prevailing modes of thought are gone.   The poet who reflects these changes modifying the surface of society, passes with the period he mirrors out of a nation's ken.   But beneath all transient ruffles of the surface of communities lies the substance of their unchanging nature, the permanent elements of their constitution.   The poet who builds upon that foundation is safe, and Burns built upon it.   It matters not for his fame that his humour wears not seldom the countenance of despair—despair was the atmosphere he breathed in the latter years of his life; that his laugh is often the laugh of desperation that comes at the wit's end.

It matters not that he was, as he called himself, 'the fool of his feelings and attachments.' All that is over and done, judgment has gone in his favour, and posterity will not withdraw it.

Although Burns had good reason to hate conventionalism, and hated hypocrisy in good earnest, his revolt took a passive form in a return to nature for poetical topics and treatment, and his patriotism was never thoroughly submerged in political radicalism. As with Byron, the cardinal defect in his poetry is its lack of serious aim. This, with its narrowness of compass, already noticed, place its author in the second rank of the immortals. But if Byron shares Burns' defect of a lack of serious aim, his poetic compass is vastly wider. Nothing is more characteristic of him than his puissant yet easy rule over the whole extent of the poetic realm, he is lord of broader acres in that enchanted empire than any since Shakespere's day. On the threshold of enquiry into Byron's rightful place among the poets, and the time may now be considered to have come when an unbiassed and final judgment is possible, we may consider it indisputable that, because Byron wrote with the most facile of pens, and apparently with an equal ease, drama or song, satire, epic or burlesque, it would be a serious fallacy to suppose that this range of subject represents real range of thought, and that he was a dramatist, a lyrist, a satirist, a comic and an epic poet who achieved greatness in all these departments.

By far the most famous poet of his own day, 'the grand Napoleon of the realms of rhyme,' his reputation has with the lapse of time suffered a steady diminution of its once far-shining glory. One coterie of modern critics inclines towards withholding from him altogether the sacred title of poet, preferring to clothe him with the honours of a brilliant rhetorician in verse. True it is that scarce a trace is to be found anywhere in Byron of the presence of the higher creative imagination; and the arc of thought he traverses, which at first sight seems to span the whole heaven of poetry, is found to have deceived us by the splendour of its colouring, and to be in reality of very limited length. This his most bigoted admirers will readily grant. But the most fastidious critic can never go so far as to rob either his life or his poetry of their indestructible romance and power. Facility in the use of all poetic instruments proves versatility, if not depth of mind; but the real value of Byron's life-work lies in its intensity of tone, the presence in it of a striking individuality, representing himself under various metrical disguises, but always the same striking individuality. His intellectual endowment was native to him, but at what hearth did he catch the spark that kindled into the flame of his poetic passion?

Byron's birth-lot was cast when the political and social facts of the Revolution had shattered the fair ideal of an everlasting reign of freedom that the social prophets had set up. If Burns represents the pre-revolution spirit of the more vigorous minds of his time, the spirit of intellectual adherence, not yet strung to the brink of action; if Wordsworth's and Coleridge's early life represents the ardour and emotion caught from the martial music and earth-shaking tramp of a nation's march against ancient tyrannies, Byron is the representative of disheartening reaction. The wave of joyous emotion had subsided, and with its recoil came an era of dejection and loss of faith. For a season could no man believe in the great inspiring social or moral causes; Byron was thrown back upon himself, and the burden was greater than he could bear. His moral and mental training had not been such as to qualify him for bearing it. From earliest childhood he had been unhappy and unfortunate. From the beginning his surroundings were such as to make impossible the acquisition of any just or sane views, either about himself or society, politics or religion. Quick-tempered, impulsive, fiery-hearted, he needed judicious training —he received a training that might have made an eccentric out of the most quiet-minded of boys. Prejudices resulted that took up their abode with him for life, distorted and false views that were never completely exorcised. The air of cynical misanthropy and affectation, at first assumed, partly, no doubt, as a cloak to hide the real man from the vulgar crowd of curious gazers, became quite as much a part of the man as if he had inherited them by birth. Capriciously educated in childhood by his mother and teachers, the educative discipline he met with in the world of society was no wiser or more consistent. His first book, 'Hours of Idleness,' did not give promise of a distinguished poetic future ; but there was no reason, except, perhaps, that he was a peer and a minor, for singling out its author for the pillory. Byron, was, however, equal to his own defence, and in 'English Bards and Scotch Reviewers' his wrongs were amply revenged. But that satire emphasised his quarrel with the world, and while he gloried in the part of a literary Ishmael, whose hand was against every man, he was not happy. After his travels, which reappear in poetic form in 'Childe Harold,' came the revulsion which placed him on the dizzy pinnacle of unrivalled contemporary fame. 'He woke and found himself famous.' 'The Giaour,' the 'Bride of Abydos,' 'The Corsair,' 'Lara,' 'The Hebrew Melodies,' followed in rapid succession. 'The Corsair,' was written in ten days, and fourteen thousand copies were bought in one. Each new poem was received with public excitement and rejoicing such as are accorded to the news of a great victory. This was not merely popularity and fame, it was enthusiasm, worship, devotion. But worship and devotion were exchanged for obloquy and odium, when, in 1816, he separated from his wife. In the same year he left England never to return, and 'bore through Europe the pageant of his bleeding heart.' The remainder of his life was chiefly spent in Geneva, Venice, Florence, Ravenna and Pisa; and the end came at Missolonghi.

The poetry of Byron reveals the ache that springs from a sense of the futility of life, from a sense of its grandeur when seen from afar, its pettiness when seen in the ranks. He found no moral or spiritual sustenance in the times, and fell back on his historic sense, which never failed to summon before him long bygone splendours and heroisms of dead ages. Deprived of faith in the present, he transferred his allegiance to 'the lost causes and forsaken beliefs and impossible loyalties' of Europe's earlier days. It was perhaps this historic sense that had to do with the final deliverance of his own soul from the thraldom of self. Into the battle for the deliverance of Greece, fallen from her ancient high estate, and under the barbaric despotism of the Turk, he flung himself at the last, when he had learnt the lesson that a life of pleasure produces only satiety, that memories of a stirring and nobler past, with no counterpart in the present, awake at best only an emotion that must end in gloom, and that self-sacrifice and devotion to some cause, whose appeal is to man's higher instinct, is imperative, if life is to be worthy, nay, even tolerable.

During the years of exile Byron produced all the more

important and mature of his poems; not one of which is free from the affectation of scorn, the false note of theatrical contempt for mankind, and what mankind most loves and desires. His poems are a record of his own personal emotions, or what he regarded as ideal emotions, a record of his own feelings placed in various environments, and of the actions he imagined would have been his own in like situations. Needless it is to say that this affectation interferes with the sincerity, the absolute truthfulness which are indispensable to the best poetry. Only when Byron expresses actual and not pretended or imagined feeling is he really great. His emotions were strong and deep, and when he utters these strong and deep emotions in the splendid style which came so easily to him, it is then that he is at his best. As imitator of Pope, or when defying in disdain and lofty scorn the powers of heaven, the affected Byron speaks; the real man as well as the true poet in that part of his work which is a record of the truth of his own personal and emotional experience.

Poetry is neither more nor less than an effort to ascertain and appropriately set forth in words those truths and beauties which human nature has the power to appreciate so far as to profit by them, truths and beauties lifted above time and place; or to simplify the expression, since 'Beauty is truth, and truth is beautiful,' 'truths not individual and local, but general and operative,' the discovery of which is a benefit not to a class or a community, but to the whole race, because they are capable of direct relation with life. Hence it comes that the more human the poetry, the more, other things being equal, its effectiveness and its durability. The question to ask concerning a poet is 'What is the value of his work for life?' The more comprehensively and the more truthfully he sees

life, the more service can he render to his fellows; and every
poet is eventually ranked according to the moral, intel-
lectual, or spiritual service he has wrought for mankind.
Hence the weakness of that poetry which is beautiful only
by reason of a deft arrangement of syllable and pause,
word and rhyme.   Hence the weakness of that poetry
which, like much of Shelley's, is often beautiful by reason
of its quaint conceits, its ingenious and fertile imagery, but
which fails to connect itself by any vital process with life.
Take a fine passage from 'Adonais,' a poem which exhibits
Shelley at his best, when least intoxicated with delight in
unreal abstractions, and compare it with passages in which
the human element is the motive force—

> ' And others came—Desires and Adorations,
>   Wingèd Persuasions and veiled Destinies,·
> Splendours and Glooms, and glimmering Incarnations
>   Of Hopes and Fears, and twilight Phantasies.' . . .

Recollecting that to dilate the imagination is to do intel-
lectual and spiritual service, and admitting that this is fine
poetry, let us ask, How does it compare with

> ' Let me not to the marriage of true minds
>   Admit impediments.   Love is not love
> Which alters where it alteration finds,
>   Or bends with the remover to remove; '

or with

> ' Only the actions of the just
> Smell sweet and blossom in their dust; '

or with

> ' Hence, in a season of calm weather,
>   Though inland far we be,
> Our souls have sight of that immortal sea
>   That brought us hither; '

or with Shelley himself—

> ' IIe has outsoared the shadow of our night,
> Envy and calumny, and hate and pain,
> And that unrest which men miscall delight,
> Can touch him not and torture not again.
> From the contagion of the world's slow stain
> IIe is secure.'

In these we hear the human voice, the accent of man's speech in his highest and most serious moods.

The poetry of Byron achieves but occasionally that high and rare beauty which consists in perfect truthfulness of substance, united with perfect fitness of expression. Not seldom is it false in emotion and disfigured by feebleness and carelessness in expression; but it is kept alive by its daring and fervour and its occasional rise to weighty magnificence and felicity of diction. It may be noted that there were two qualities of which he was entirely destitute. He had no critical faculty and he had no dramatic faculty. Although the revolution in poetry from the style of Pope had been begun and carried on by several poets before the meteoric suddenness and brilliancy of Byron's appearance, and although he was destined to do valiantly in the struggle for the emancipation of the Muses from their bondage of over a hundred years in the prison of pseudo-classicism, in theory Byron was an adherent of the classical school. For Pope his reverence was unbounded, and of himself he spoke as guilty of contributing to the destruction of right principles in poetry. 'As to Pope, I have always regarded him as the greatest name in our poetry. Depend upon it, the rest are barbarians.' Such is the influence of style. And again, 'All the styles of the day are bombastic. I don't except my own; no one has done more through negligence

to corrupt the language.' Forced by circumstances into the
ranks of the revolutionists in poetry, though he did magnifi-
cent service, he was never convinced of the greatness or
justice of the cause. When it is added that he preferred
his own poor imitations of Pope to 'Childe Harold,' nothing
need be added to prove that Byron's literary judgment was
so unreliable as to be utterly worthless. In respect of his
want of dramatic faculty, Macaulay has clearly enough made
good his dictum. That Byron was never at home in the
management of dialogue is significant. He cannot support
it for any reasonable period; it is without life or movement.
Monologue was his instrument. 'Childe Harold' and the
other sustained poems are monologues with Byron in
various masks as chief speaker. Even to 'Manfred'—far
the finest of his essays at dramatic form—the same descrip-
tion applies. The sentiment never varies. The melancholy
figure of the disdainful hero stalks through them all, and
we know his attitudes; one poem makes us familiar with
them. The scene may differ, the plot may develop
differently, but there can be no mistaking the gloomy face
which looks, or affects to look, upon the world as its enemy.
Such an iron limitation it is sufficient to indicate. We may
then be satisfied that by far the greater part of Byron's
poetry is destitute of the qualities which ensure a permanent
popularity. Much remains to bid defiance to time; what
are its distinctive excellences? It must first be observed
that Byron is of another order of poets than those who are
the present gods of the people. 'We are now accustomed,'
as Mr Symonds told us, ' to the art which appeals to edu-
cated sensibilities by suggestions and reflections, by careful
workmanship and attentive study of form, by carefully-
finished epitomes of feeling, by picturesquely-blended re-

miniscences of realism, culture, and poetical idealism.' It
is but natural that to minds trained to delight in the de-
tailed fine strokes of miniature painting neither the methods
nor the effects of Byron are suited, for he is a painter upon a
large canvas, who uses broad brushes and clear, vivid pig-
ments.   He did not care for minute accuracies of outline,
for faint delicacies of colouring; but preferred bold and
large designs, well-defined chiaroscuro, and free and daring
handling.   The almost morbid spirit of introspection that
reigns over the whole of modern poetry, the subtile analysis
to which each and all of our later poets call us, the meta-
physical or other gospels of which almost without exception
they are apostles, none of these things belongs to Byron.
His is, if anything, a poetry of action, of movement, and of
scene and incident; its energy is the energy of passion;
modern poetry lives on reflection, analysis, detail, studied
elaboration of diction.   The greatness of 'Childe Harold'
does not lie in occasional delicate felicities of phrase or
idea, but in the grandeur of its rapid succession of pictures,
the vast extent of its scheme, and the sonorous march of its
flowing versification.   Marred as many of the finest pas-
sages are by looseness of construction, commonplaceness of
thought, and even lapses from grammar, the eloquence
which sustains such a weight of subject as the scenery and
history of half the countries of Europe is not matched in
the poetry of every century.

Take a stanza from the description of Venice as an
example of his style.

> ' I stood in Venice, on the Bridge of Sighs ;
> A palace and a prison on each hand :
> I saw from out the wave her structures rise
> As from the stroke of the enchanter's wand :

A thousand years their cloudy wings expand
Around me, and a dying glory smiles
O'er the far times when many a subject land
Look'd to the wingèd lion's marble piles
Where Venice sat in state, thron'd on her hundred isles.'

Fairly representative as this is of the general poetic level
of 'Childe Harold,' it cannot be praised as high poetry,
and yet few will read it without pleasure.   To sustain
a very long poem at this elevation is indisputably a poetic
feat, perhaps a greater feat than the carving of a gem.
But when Byron is really roused, when his imagination
is fired, he can do better than this.   Usually the imagina-
tion has little to do with the historic recollections of
Europe in 'Childe Harold;' but at times it flashes a
scene, or a series of scenes, in a few swift lines with
splendid energy.

'Last noon beheld them full of lusty life,
Last eve, in beauty's circle proudly gay,
The midnight brought the signal-sound of strife,
The morn the marshalling in arms,—the day
Battle's magnificently stern array !
The thunder-clouds close o'er it, which when rent
The earth is covered thick with other clay,
Which her own clay shall cover, heaped and pent,
Rider and horse—friend, foe—in one red burial blent.'

The compressed fire and force of poetry like this must
disarm criticism.   Like Pope, Byron 'lisped in numbers for
the numbers came.'   He was only nineteen when he pub-
lished 'Hours of Idleness.'   Neither in subject matter nor
in manner did it give promise of the author's poetic future,
nor of the power that was to come.   He was trying his hand,
but had not yet found the weapons suited to it.   'English
Bards and Scotch Reviewers' revealed something of the satiric

humour afterwards so conspicuously displayed ; but it was in 'Childe Harold,' when he became the poetic chronicler of Spain and of Greece, of Switzerland and of Italy, that Byron made claim to be the chief of the living English poets. Scott, in the vivid narratives of the north country, of Border skirmish and Highland warfare, had given a new impulse to the treatment of epic subjects in modern poetry. The public taste had thus been educated in this style, and Byron took advantage of the education to write tale after tale, whose incident and passion, set forth in powerful declamatory verse, thrilled and held captive the imagination of the time. These tales are now little read. Based though they were upon accurate observation, for Byron's imagination, unlike Shelley's, could never dispense with material, though each is a magnificent *tour de force*, their qualities are not such as rightly distinguish poetry, just as the qualities of Pope's work, although admirable, are not the qualities which make poetry either great or enduring. In 'Beppo,' and supremely in 'Don Juan,' a side of Byron's genius displays itself in unique and splendid fashion. John Hookham Frere's 'Whistlecraft' was, he tells us, his model. Elsewhere in English poetry we shall look in vain for a vein of humour at once so original, caustic, ironical and inexhaustible. As he passes, in a moment, from grave to gay, from the sincerest passion and pathos to ironic or burlesque humour, we feel that we are under the hand of a master, and that master the strangely noble and impetuously generous, the strangely vulgar and deliberately mean, the fool of conflicting forces who redeemed his life in its latest selfhonouring resolve, the poet who was the greatest force of the century of his birth.

Matthew Arnold, while admitting that Byron was the

greatest poetic power in our literature of his own day, puts his finger, as Goethe did before him, upon the incurable weakness of his poetry. That poetry, he tells us, did not know enough ; it had its rise in a movement of feeling, not in a movement of mind. And Goethe, using a different phrase, expresses the same idea,—'The moment he reflects he is a child.' If we go through the list of the greatest poets of the world, we shall find that they retain their places at the head of the world's poetry by reason of the fact that their thought, their reflections, are of lasting value, that they were great philosophers no less than great poets. The philosophy of Byron, like the philosophy of Shelley, is without enduring or universal application. We cannot recommend to mankind the adoption of Byron's views of life, or Shelley's views of life. If mankind were to adopt them they would be nothing the better of them ; indeed, we should be wise in strenuously opposing any movement for the universal application of the theories of such poets to practical affairs. The philosophy of Sophocles, of Dante, or of Milton, we might unreservedly praise and recommend as an excellent rule whereby life might be wisely ordered ; but a philosophy of defiance such as that of Byron, or of Shelley—a philosophy of defiance without good reasons for defiance, without any basis either in accurate experience of human nature, or in just and sane reflection upon that experience, this cannot be recommended as a guide to living wisely and happily. As a French critic has said, ' Byron posed all his life long,' and from such a man we cannot expect sure moral or spiritual guidance any more than the highest poetry. In spite, then, of his wit, keen, flashing, forceful ; in spite of his splendid vigour, his 'dash, daring and grandeur '; in spite of the fact that he was, as Goethe said, ' a personality, such as for its eminence as has never been yet, and such as is not likely to come again'; despite all this, we may not assign to Byron a place in the first rank. If it be necessary to assign him a place at all and not simply content ourselves with the enjoyment of what is best in him, because he has not the intellectual grip or the sanity of Wordsworth, he must rank below him, although next to him.   But that place he is not likely ever to lose ; for whatever changes may come, however fashions may vary in criticism, there remains in Byron's poetry a source of permanent human interest, the intense utterance of an individuality of immense intellectual resource and possibility of moral grandeur, of such an individuality fallen upon evil days, suffering the life-long pain of surrender to a lower set of impulses, and gifted with a mastery over the larger, stronger effects of language unmatched before or since his time.

Vivid, free and daring as Byron's descriptions are, theirs is not the abiding and constant charm of his powerful expressions of powerful emotion.   But in these two things, in the stormy strength of his descriptions, and in the fervent delineation of fiery passions, his province is uninvaded by another.   Take an instance of each.   The first, a thunderstorm among the Alps—

> ' Far along,
> From peak to peak, the rattling crags among
> Leaps the live thunder ! not from one lone cloud,
> But every mountain now hath found a tongue,
> And Jura answers, through her misty shroud,
> Back to the joyous Alps, who call to her aloud !
>
> And this is in the night ; most glorious night !
> Thou wast not sent for slumber ! let me be

A sharer in thy fierce and far delight—
A portion of the tempest and of thee !
How the lit lake shines—a phosphoric sea—
And the big rain comes dancing to the earth !
And now again 'tis black, and now the glee
Of the loud hill shakes with its mountain-mirth,
As if they did rejoice o'er a young earthquake's birth.'

In such a description the natural energy and ecstasy of the poet's mind are fused to a fervent delight in the corresponding aspects of nature, her passion and her power. Here Byron is eminent, and again in passages where human nature displays its violent moods or suffers the final eclipse of death.

' I see before me the gladiator lie :
He leans upon his hand—his manly brow
Consents to death, but conquers agony,
And his drooped head sinks gradually low,
As through his side the last drops, ebbing slow
From the red gash, fall heavy, one by one,
Like the first of a thunder-shower ; and now
The arena swims around him—he is gone,
Ere ceased the inhuman shout which hailed the wretch who won.

' He heard it, but he heeded not—his eyes
Were with his heart, and that was far away :
He recked not of the life he lost nor prize,
But where his rude hut by the Danube lay ;
There were his young barbarians all at play,
There was their Dacian mother—he, their sire,
Butchered to make a Roman holiday.'

The imaginative truth of a picture such as this forces itself upon every reader, and retains for it a place in the gallery of the things that are permanent intellectual treasures.

No one is in a position to determine the value of such word-painting as Byron's, who has not come to recognise what has been called the 'pictorial powerlessness of language.' * 'The beauty or the truth of Titian's flesh tint,' says Mr Ruskin, 'can be appreciated by all, but it is only to the artist, whose multiplied hours of toil have not reached the slightest resemblance to one of its tones, that its *excellence* is manifest.' The difficulty of quickening language out of its powerlessness, of breathing into it a life which no word or random combination of words possesses, and no mere toil can achieve, this is where the genius of the artist is exhibited. Byron's art did not at all consist in the weaving of subtle harmonies, in the marshalling of musical syllables, it consisted rather in the production of broad and striking effects. By the breadth and strength of his descriptive treatment, by the grandeur of his scheme, he is high among the artists, although, perhaps, he had little or no ear for the finer word-cadences, the delicate melodies that intoxicate the sense in Keats or Coleridge or Tennyson. His work gives the impression that all rapid work upon large subjects must give. It exhibits carelessness of detail, but boldness in seizing and power in grouping the striking features, the lines of force in landscape, scene or character.

The office of the poet has always been regarded as two-fold. We think of him not only as maker or artist, but as prophet or revealer. When the enquiry suggests itself wherein lay Byron's message to his age, the spiritual significance of his poetry, we find ourselves at a loss. Is it possible that so great a man has left no enduring word of help or of consolation to his fellow-men? Attention

* Professor Dowden.

has often been directed to the fact that, above all other literatures, that produced by the English race has been conspicuous for its moral purpose.   The makers of our literature have been almost without exception men who took a serious view of life, who felt it to be a responsible burden. But like the men of the Restoration period, Byron never took upon himself this burden of duty, never felt called upon to remain at some post alloted by the gods.   If he were possessed of any moral purpose, that purpose had little effect upon his course of life, and it does not appear in his poetry.   There is not to be found even the calm stoicism of such a sentiment as this—

> ' Men must endure
> Their going hence even as their coming hither ;
> Ripeness is all.'

Much less the serene patience of—

> ' They also serve who only stand and wait ; '

or the sublime confidence in moral ends of Plato—' This then must be our notion of the just man that, even when he is in poverty or sickness, or any other seeming mis-fortune, all things will in the end work together for good to him in life or death ; for the gods have a care of any-one whose desire is to become just and to be like God, as far as man can attain the divine likeness by the pursuit of virtue.'   These are messages of cheer to the human race, but Byron does not encourage us by the music of any such strain towards higher spiritual attainments.   How far does the absence of this strain of moral purpose militate against the greatness of his poetry, and how is it to be accounted for ?   It is to be accounted for by his attitude of revolt. The cause of the absence of spiritual or moral tone from the poetry of the Restoration lay in the fact that the attitude of the minds of that era was one of revolt—revolt against the absurd and unnatural strictness, the cramping influences of the Puritan creed. The reaction against Puritanism went too far, as is the tendency of reactions. But such a reaction as that of the Restoration, although productive of a season of spiritual unfruitfulness, is in the end salutary, helpful to the nation and to the individual. The case of Byron is a parallel one. In the society of his day he met with the formalities of religion but little real faith, hope and charity; abundance of pretence and of falsehood, abundance of insincerity, of shallow thinking and selfish living. He found a society fettered by self-imposed rules and restrictions, which were without meaning or rationality, and against this slavery he revolted. His attitude, as was natural, was made more determined by the treatment the society he despised accorded him. The estrangement became open war. In his poems Byron waged war without truce or discrimination against the conventional religion, the conventional political opinions, the conventional social views of his age. Fierce against these shams, in the vehemence of his hatred he was carried away to excesses more violent than wise. The reaction intensified by his own sufferings—for Byron truly suffered—carried him too far, and much of the divine fire of his genius expended itself in consuming with ridicule all that the age felt or pretended to feel most sacred. Not in his poems only but in his life Byron maintained his defiant port, making a derision of all the rules sanctioned by the traditions and experience of preceeding generations. He lived fast and recklessly, and wrote poems glorifying a fast and reckless life. From such a poet no hand is stretched in the service of an upward toiling humanity. There is then no *positive* moral purpose in Byron. But is it therefore to be said that his work is vain, a hindrance rather than a gain to the generations that come after him? Such conclusion would be unwarrantable. There is a *negative* moral purpose. The prophets of God were not seldom in wrathful mood, filled with holy indignation at the wickedness and the idolatries of the people. The moral purpose to be seen in Byron is moral purpose in a destructive, in a wrathful mood. The endeavour to purify heart and mind must begin with the eradication of the tendencies in human nature to self-deceit, to a blinding self-complaisance. Byron saw clearly enough that the England of his day was in the strong prison of an invincible or almost invincible ignorance; and because he shook the citadel of that ignorance to its foundations, a portion of the prophetic revealing gift, which has belonged to the poets by divine right, is his also.

In speaking of Byron reference should never be omitted to the service he rendered not to his own nation alone but to Europe in drawing all eyes to English literature. Shakespere excepted, there is no other with an equal European reputation. In the eloquent phrase of Mazzini, 'He led the genius of Britain on a pilgrimage throughout all Europe.' His splendid name, coupled with the celebrity that attached to it when he joined the Greek army of independence, an act productive of unbounded enthusiasm, were the sufficient causes of his European renown.

Among the poets of Revolution the name of Ebenezer Elliott, the corn-law rhymer cannot be passed over, and he may be mentioned with Byron for two reasons. Elliott's

poetry deals with large subjects with a like passion, and
his imagination never leaves earth, but is always in touch
with concrete fact. When his soul is in arms he has
something of the same voice, the voice of Tyrtæus.

> ' Day, like our souls, is fiercely dark,
>   What then? 'tis day !
> We sleep no more ; the cock crows—hark !
>   To arms, away ! '

In his shorter poems, when he attempted condensation,
Byron was not always successful; rarely happy, indeed, except
when free to range over great tracts ; but he has left a few
masterpieces in a more restrained style. We must always
remember that, like his contemporaries, Shelley and Keats,
he died a very young man, at the age of thirty-six. Crowded
and vigorous as that life was, and crowned with marvellous
poetic achievement, we may be sure that had he lived his
poetry would have gained, if not in strength, certainly in
other and even greater qualities. To anyone who doubts
that it would have been so no better answer can be given
than the last poem written on the completion of his thirty-
sixth birthday at Missolonghi, three months before the end
came. It marks the dawn of a nobler resolution than ever
before beautified his life.

> ' The sword, the banner, and the field,
>   Glory and Greece, around me see !
> The Spartan borne upon his shield,
>   Was not more free.
>
> Awake ! (not Greece—she *is* awake !)
>   Awake, my spirit ! Think through *whom*
> Thy life-blood tracks its parent lake,
>   And then strike home.

Tread those reviving passions down,
    Unworthy manhood ; unto thee
Indifferent should the smile or frown
    Of beauty be.

If thou regrett'st thy youth, why live?
    The land of honourable death
Is here :—up to the field, and give
    Away thy breath !

Seek out—less often sought than found—
    A soldier's grave, for thee the best ;
Then look around, and choose thy ground
    And take thy rest.'

In that 'land of honourable death' he died on the 19th
of April 1824.

CHAPTER IV

NATURALISM AND SUPERNATURALISM IN POETRY

Coleridge—Wordsworth—Lamb—Bowles

THE restless passion for a perfection to be consummated here and now, which brought about the political and social changes of the Revolution, brought about also the movement named 'transcendental.' A desire for the absolute in action led in the latter years of the eighteenth century to the materialistic revolution, whose spiritual counterpart, a corresponding desire for the absolute in thought, led to the new and enlarged conceptions which drew Nature and man closer to their infinite source. The eighteenth century, an intellectual but unimaginative period in the history of civilisation, made relative truth its object, and regarded 'probability,' in Bishop Butler's phrase, 'as the very guide of life.' If the materialistic revolution be read aright, it will be read as an effort to translate the newly liberated ideals of the spirit of man into instant practice. This was the outcome of the new spirit in the sphere of political philosophy. Transcendental thought in the sphere of metaphysical philosophy aimed at an overthrow of the mechanical procedure of the empirical thinkers, and the substitution of the science of real knowledge, not derived mediately through the senses but immediately from the central fountain of being. Relative truth, tolerable, social and political institutions were no longer satisfying, and were henceforth discredited. For the future there was to be no rest for the soul; for it could never again make its home amid relative truths and tolerable social and political institutions. Looking back towards the opening of the century, Wordsworth and Coleridge seem to stand over against each other, the two pillars of Hercules at the entrance to the boundless ocean of the new world, over which the hunger of the heart for a stainless ideal drives the child of our unquiet time on a quest which he cannot relinquish, though he knows it will be vain.

Wordsworth's friendship with Coleridge, the strong bond between them in their early days of work, rendered memorable by the joint authorship of the 'Lyrical Ballads,' has made their name and fame inseparable. And yet the extreme diversity in character and temperament of these two men is at once apparent. They visited Germany together in early life, and the influences of that visit are significant of the type of mind of each. Wordsworth made little way in the acquisition of the language, remained undisturbed by the influx of any fresh stream of ideas, and continued quietly to give himself almost wholly to the composition of his own poems. Not even in later life did he express any reverence for Goethe; and the philosophers failed to attract him. Coleridge plunged immediately into the metaphysical studies with which he occupied so large a portion of his life, and did so much to forward in England. The truth is, Wordsworth's faiths were never arrived at by logical process. They were the result of meditative contemplation which brooded on and on, until thought died away into feeling, and the contemplation ceased to be in

any degree intellectual, and became purely impassioned
It was by an undivided single process that his distinctive
creed was developed.   No mind reaches by logic a con-
clusion such as this :—

> 'And 'tis my faith that every flower
> Enjoys the air it breathes.'

Coleridge's mind, on the other hand, was characterised
by a ratiocinative meditativeness, he was fully conscious of
the steps of demonstration by which his faiths were estab-
lished.   His belief was dependent upon intellectual assent.
The abiding peace of heart that distinguished Wordsworth's
whole life sprang from that same quiet acquisition of a
faith not learnt in the schools, but which unfolded and
expanded out of the bosom of solitary meditation.
Coleridge's disquiet was the no less natural outcome of a
creed born amid contention, and at any moment liable to
attack or overthrow from suspected or unsuspected quarters.
Poetry, which was to him, as he has himself told us, 'its
own exceeding great reward,' was far from being, as Words-
worth's poetry was, the direct and natural expression of his
complete character and life.   Coleridge's was a far more
complex character and less uniform life, and poetry was
Coleridge's refuge, the land of dreams into which he could
make his escape, the writing of which could 'give him
pleasure,' as he said, ' when nothing else could.'
    While, then, we may read Wordsworth with perfect
confidence that we are in communion with the poet's very
self, we know that only a part of Coleridge, only the
dreamer of strange dreams, who has escaped from the
philosopher close clasped in the metaphysical coil, only a
part of the whole man is with us.   This is the clue to the

fragmentary and sensuous character of his best poems. They do not embody his philosophy of life, only the phantasies of his visionary hour. Yet these pleasure excursions into the rich demesne of the pure imagination will preserve the name of Coleridge when the note-books which represent the intellectual wealth of his mind, and the influences that radiated from it, are only known to the student. In the storm and stress of the conflicts of time, names are forgotten that once were in all men's mouths : others never spoken, save by their friends, may emerge into sudden fame perhaps a hundred years after the gravestones recorded them apparently for the last time. Reputation is a strange thing, and it would be unwise to count on posthumous honours. Milton, the poet, was little known in his own day. Milton, the political controversialist, was so famous that he came near to suffering severely for his part in the support of Cromwellianism. The years have changed all that. Coleridge, 'the Seer of Highgate,' 'the rapt one of the god-like forehead,' who seemed in his own day the speaker of the oracular words concerning human life and the mysteries surrounding it, this Coleridge has passed away, and the Coleridge of the 'Ancient Mariner' and 'Christabel,' the poet alone remains. With the philosophical Coleridge we have here no concern, especially since his philosophy and his poetry are not inextricably blended as they were with Wordsworth. Indeed, what must first strike the reader of Coleridge's poetry is its independence of the time which produced it. Save for the few political odes there is almost nothing which bears unmistakable marks of the era of its birth. The dawn of Romanticism is there plainly visible, the first ripple of the wave which at last broke and spent itself in pre-Raphaelite art, but intellectual

kinship between the 'Ancient Mariner' and the opening
of the century there is none. A very refined and subtle
criticism might find in Coleridge's poems dealing with
supernatural subjects something of the modern psycholo-
gical spirit.   It is surely nearer the truth to regard them as
detached from any movement of thought, and joined to
their birth-time by the slender link of a renewed delight in
ballad literature and mediæval sentiment. 'Christabel' and
'The Ancient Mariner' are poems of absolute originality,
owing nothing in matter or manner to any previous poet.
The imagination at work in them is imagination working
upon a single hint, and the artist in verse has learned from
these poems a hundred times more than ever their author
learned from another. William Lisle Bowles, the poet-
canon of Salisbury, was the god of his youthful idolatry;
but it was not long ere he surpassed his model, who must
rank, however, as graceful sonneteer, and even true poet,
though his vein was of the slenderest.   Coleridge, as we
have been told, was an epicure in sound, and who can
doubt it?   The exquisite vowel-music of 'Christabel,' its
delicate modulations and magic suggestiveness breathe the
very spirit of a vision of enchantment.   Here, and in
'Kubla Khan,' the subtlest effects of this the greatest
English metrical artist since Milton, were obtained; an
artist who, like Milton, was a careful workman, conscious
not only of the beauty of the results of his skill, but of how
the results were arrived at.   With Wordsworth it was
different.   While the richness of the melodies of Coleridge
is wanting to him, his music, where there is music at all,
is less sensuous, more bracing, and usually born of an
inspiring idea which seemed, without the poet's conscious
guidance, to build itself a lasting home of perfect sound.

The 'Lyrical Ballads,' in which the public first became acquainted with the rime of the 'Ancient Mariner,' were published in 1798. 'The thought suggested itself,' Coleridge writes in his 'Biographia Literaria,' 'that a series of poems might be composed of two sorts. In the one the incidents and agents were to be, in part at least, supernatural, and the excellence aimed at was to consist in interesting the affections by the dramatic truth of such emotions as would naturally accompany such situations, supposing them real. And real in this sense they have been to every human being, who, from whatever source of delusion, has at any time believed himself under divine agency. For the second class, subjects were to be chosen from ordinary life—the characters and incidents were to be such as will be found in every village and its vicinity where there is a meditative and feeling mind to seek after them, or to notice them when they present themselves. In this idea originated the plan of the ' Lyrical Ballads '; in which it was agreed that my endeavours should be directed to persons and characters supernatural, or at least romantic ; yet so as to transfer from our inward nature a human interest and a resemblance of truth sufficient to procure for these shadows of imagination that willing suspension of disbelief for the moment which constitutes poetic faith. Now, Wordsworth, on the other hand, was to propose to himself as his object, to give the charm of novelty to things of every day, and to excite a feeling analogous to the supernatural by awakening the mind's attention from the lethargy of custom, and directing it to the loveliness and the wonders of the world before us ; an inexhaustible treasure, but for which, in consequence of the film of familiarity and selfish solicitude, we have eyes yet see not, ears that hear not, and hearts that neither feel nor understand.' In this finely suggestive passage we have the most succinct exposition of the individual mission which Wordsworth and Coleridge set before themselves in poetry, and to which each consistently adhered. The suspension of disbelief for the moment, which constitutes poetic faith, is very artfully brought about by Coleridge in the 'Ancient Mariner.' The ship, whose adventure we follow, sets sail for familiar seas, but ere we are aware her reckoning is lost, and her keel ploughs an enchanted ocean unknown to the geographers. The illusion is perfect, because at no point is there any rude surprise awaiting us. The incidents of an ordinary voyage glide imperceptibly into the marvellous, the natural and the supernatural mingle like homogeneous elements. Since Shakespere there was no such natural supernaturalism in English poetry. Spenser opens the wicket gate with his magic key, and we are straight in Fairyland; Milton transports us bodily to another world; but with Coleridge, while even now we have the green and solid earth beneath our feet, we look up and down, the mystic light has fallen around us, and the miracle has been wrought.

The running prose commentary that accompanies the poem displays the same sweet and delicate tone as his most musical verse, and the same dreamy richness of fancy. It were difficult to say whether there be any stanza in 'The Ancient Mariner' so truly of the finest poetic texture as the gloss upon the lines—

'The moving moon went up the sky,
    And nowhere did abide;
Softly she was going up,
    And a star or two beside;'

where the unuttered emotion of the mariner's heart at the sight is thus exquisitely suggested :—

'In his loneliness and fixedness he yearneth towards the journeying moon, and the stars that still sojourn, yet still move onward ; and everywhere the blue sky belongs to them, and is their appointed rest, and their native country, and their own natural homes, which they enter unannounced, as lords that are certainly expected, and yet there is a silent joy at their arrival.'

The poet Coleridge was but a part of the man, of whom, perhaps, the major part was philosopher—'logician, metaphysician, bard,' as Charles Lamb in one of his happy phrases described him.   And because poetry was not the serious business of his life, it has not the sustaining, spirit-enriching power that belongs to poetry that grapples with the graver issues.   But Coleridge's nature was one which vibrated to every breath of beauty ; and he has so rendered his impressions, with such exactness and such winning grace, that his poetry, while not stimulative to thought in such a high degree as Wordsworth's, equals it in educative influence upon the feelings.   The best of his poems would serve admirably as touchstones for determining a reader's apprehension of the finer shades of felicitous poetic expression. Few as are the songs he has left us of

'High and passionate thought
To their own music chanted,'

the golden richness of his cadences, the tender purity of his feeling, the firmness and delicacy of his touch in rendering Nature, the mystic halo that envelops it, these make his best poetry more like inspired incantation than the work of any mortal.   Take almost any passage from 'Christabel' to represent all these qualities, or this, where the Mariner listens to the celestial music of a troop of angelic spirits—

F

> ' And now 'twas like all instruments,
> Now like a lonely flute ;
> And now it is an angel's song
> That makes the heavens be mute.
>
> It ceased ; yet still the sails made on
> A pleasant noise till noon—
> A noise like of a hidden brook
> In the leafy month of June,
> That to the sleeping woods all night
> Singeth a quiet tune.'

Coleridge is one of the few poets who have been successful in communicating to their verse the power of awakening in the mind the eerie sense, the uneasy conviction of invisible presences inhabiting lonely places—

> ' Like one that on a lonesome road,
> Doth walk in fear and dread,
> And, having once turned round, walks on,
> And turns no more his head ;
> Because he knows a frightful fiend
> Doth close behind him tread.'

Master of poetics as Coleridge was, it is natural that, as critic, his work should be penetrative and stimulating. We may regard him as the head and chief of the school of criticism which is exegetical rather than magisterial, interpretative rather than judicial. With Coleridge the court of criticism became for the first time not a court of legal but of scientific investigation. The fixed standards of Johnson, the classic precedents so long quoted as final by the professional reviewer, were now set aside, and, as the equity administered by the Supreme Court of Appeal varies according to the Chancellor's conscience, the literary conscience of Coleridge made sweeping reform of justice in the republic of letters. To his sagacity is due the rescue of criticism

from the not unmerited censure that its decisions were con-
sistently reversed by later generations, and its reinstatement
as an important official department of State.   Criticism has
often been a blind leading of the blind.   True criticism is
not that which calls attention to its own brilliancy or subtlety,
but which obtains for the author criticised a more widespread
and a more intelligent appreciation.

It is interesting to remember that the first poems of one
of the most truly gifted of English critics, Charles Lamb,
appeared in a volume of Coleridge.   ' My friend Lloyd and
myself,' he wrote, ' came into our first battle under cover of
the greater Ajax.'   But Lamb's name is secure from oblivion
for other reasons than that he was Coleridge's friend.
Perhaps he shares with Goldsmith the enviable lot of being
' the best beloved of English writers.'

The misleading appellation of the ' Lake School ' has
fostered the impression that a bond of similar poetic
methods united Wordsworth, Southey and Coleridge.   We
have seen that it was not so.   Beyond a renewed love of
Nature, fuller and deeper than that of any previous poet,
there is little in the poetry of one of this band of friends to
remind us of another.   And even here Coleridge is but an
acolyte who swings a perfumed censer in her honour :
Wordsworth, the true priest of Nature, for her law was
engraved upon his heart, and he knew the language of her
matins and her vespers.

We cannot call the beginning of the century, to which
these, together with the other great poets of the time
belonged, an epoch of serene mental temper.   It was agi-
tated with strong emotions, swayed by new and powerful
ideas, filled to overflowing with all that can awaken en-
thusiasm and nerve sustained or excited action.   We cannot

say of the poets that they surmounted its turmoil of stormy
movements. Coleridge, Byron, Shelley, felt its storm and
stress, and mirrored it in splendid fashion. One alone, the
greatest of them, experienced its excitement, sounded its
depths, and none the less possessed his own soul in
peace.

The splendid personality of the author of ' Childe Harold '
attracted all eyes, and the confessions of that personality
were read by the England of his day with a feverish eager-
ness. The personality of Wordsworth drew no public
attention. A retiring student of Nature, whose life had no
special interest to his countrymen, he meditated and com-
posed poems in solitude, which were neglected by all but
a few admirers, and were greeted by the critics with a tem-
pest of ridicule. Three things were against any genial
acceptance of Wordsworth's early poems—the unfamiliar
poetic ground broken in them, the apparent triviality of
their subject-matter, and the apparent feebleness of their
form. His juvenile poems passed unnoticed, but when he
put forth, in the second edition of the 'Lyrical Ballads,' a
poetic theory to prove their excellent qualities, the scornful
mirth of the public was no longer repressible. That poetic
theory asserted that the diction of poetry and the diction of
prose were one and the same, and that poetry was merely
' a metrical arrangement of the real language of men in a
state of vivid sensation.' The poems which followed the
preface setting forth this theory were supposed to be illus-
trative of its truth, a verification of the principles elaborated
by the author. The merits of Wordsworth's best poetry
have now come to be universally admitted, but the original
position taken up was considerably modified by the poet
himself, criticised in a friendly spirit by Coleridge, and

while now regarded as full of suggestion, and as an important contribution towards the elucidation of the true principles of poetic composition, has been set aside as far from complete or final.   In his early poems, Wordsworth departed a very short way from the poetic forms of his predecessors; he began in the school of Pope. There is, perhaps, evidence in them to a discerning eye, like that of Coleridge, of the dawn of a new day, but they wear the outward semblance of the poetry of the Augustan age. The poetry of the eighteenth century was unsatisfying. Wordsworth felt that it was unsatisfying, and he made enquiry into the causes. With Pope and his successors, thoughts, which might have been well and forcibly expressed in prose, were made poetical by the use of an ornate diction designed to hide the common-place character of the subject-matter; prosaic and obvious ideas were tricked out in the gala-dress of an artificial language, and were thus suffered to pass as really poetic and new. Wordsworth saw clearly enough that no such deception was effectual, that prose could not be transferred into poetry by the employment of a more ornate vocabulary, that prose could in no wise be translated into poetry; employ what words you will, arrange your rhymes as deftly as you will, prose will remain prose. It follows, then, that if the language of poetry in no way necessarily differs from the language of prose, except that it is metrically arranged, we must seek for the difference between prose and poetry, or rather between matter of fact or science and poetry, either in the thought or in the way it is conveyed. Wordsworth puts the essential point in this way: 'The poet thinks and feels in the spirit of human passions;' and the task he set himself was to seek for genuine human emotions, and to express them in the simplest and most direct language metrically arranged. And here we may return to a point touched in the introductory chapter, and glance at a cause of Wordsworth's frequent failure. The function of prose and the function of poetry differ very widely. The right function of prose is exposition, and its aim is to convince, to persuade. The subjects dealt with may be new, or old set forth in a new light and it may be with additional knowledge. The range of prose is a much wider one than the range of poetry; no subject is excluded from treatment in prose; in poetry the subject-matter, no less than the manner of its treatment, is of a special kind; there is much which cannot enter the charmed circle. And this is so because the function of poetry is to set forth ideas of universal interest as seen by an individual mind, and its exposition must be such as to convey pleasure. Prose may effect its object without pleasing; poetry that does not please is disarmed of its weapon of attack upon the mind, into which it is accustomed to make its way and carry its message, not by any rude storming of the citadel, such as prose may attempt, but by charm of words and subtle heart-subduing cadences, which are of such magical efficacy that the gates of the mind immediately open to it, reminding us how the walls of Jericho fell down flat, simply at the sound of the trumpet. Wordsworth forgot at times that the ideas with which the poet deals must be ideas of universal interest, and that poetry, to be efficacious, must please. The ideas upon which some of his poems are built are ideas or incidents of merely personal interest.

> ' I've watched you now a full half-hour,
> Self-poised upon that yellow flower ;
> And, little butterfly ! indeed
> I know not if you sleep or feed ; '

and sometimes his verse lacks the essential quality, and is
not pleasure-giving.

> ' Few months of life has he in store,
> As he to you will tell,
> For still the more he works, the more
> Do his weak ankles swell.'

It needs not to enquire how far the real language of men is
the true language of poetry, and how far Wordsworth
employed it.   It is not exclusively the true language of
poetry, and Wordsworth did not exclusively employ it.
The assertion that the every-day language of the rustic, as
nearest of all men to nature, even cleansed of provincialism,
is superior to that spoken. by cultivated men, is to make the
mistake that there is only one kind of conventionalism, the
polite, and that there is not a vulgar conventionalism of speech
likewise.   But against the conventionalism of an artificial
poetic diction Wordsworth was justified in setting his face,
and right, too, in believing that in poetry living and
natural language was to be preferred.   In practice he by
no means held by his extreme theory, and erred rather in
the exaggeration than in the original conception of its
principles.   In later life he came to recognise the incom-
municable majesty of a style like that of Virgil or of Milton,
which has nothing in common with the real language of the
rustic, and nothing in common with the diction of prose.

But Wordsworth's warfare was holy, because it was a
warfare against a more blighting conventionalism than that
of poetic diction, of which that was merely an outward
symptom, the conventionalism of the heart and mind, of
the very man himself.   He saw that over the natural man
the traditions and habits of his environment formed a crust,
that his real emotions and thoughts had no free play, that

his true spirit gradually died within him, and his behaviour
came to be dictated and regulated by influences external to
himself, when

> ' Custom lay upon him with a weight
> Heavy as frost, and deep almost as life.'

In his search for the simple elemental feelings and pas-
sions he concluded that among the rustic population, who
lived freer, plainer lives than the inhabitants of cities, these
might best be found.   The natural man, it is true, will be
transformed by city life into a more restrained, artificial
being.

> ' In yonder social mill
> We rub each other's angles down,
> And merge . . . in form and gloss
> The picturesque in man and man.'

The question may be interposed by someone whether
the north-country dalesman, whom Wordsworth believed
the least transformed and most childlike of men, in the
sense of most unaffected and natural, is in reality nearer to
nature's original type ; but we may take it the poet's instinct
did not wholly deceive him, and that his effort to discover the
real man behind the mask, that all men sooner or later wear,
was rightly applied.   In this effort, as well as in the effort
to express his thought and emotion with scrupulous direct-
ness and truthfulness, in the most unaffected and purest
language which admitted of metrical arrangement, he was
more than partially successful.   There is no purer, more
direct, more forcible diction than Wordsworth's when he is
at his best.   No English poet since his day has come as
near the Greek ideal of perfection in art, a chastened plain-
ness.   'The excellence of diction,' to go back again to
Aristotle, who is, after all, a surer guide than most modern

critics ; ‘ the excellence of diction consists in being perspicu-
ous without being mean.’   The distinctive characteristic
of pure art is the avoidance of any lines in the drawing
of an object save those which clearly outline it.   Tennyson
and Keats, although they at times approach the classic
severity of Wordsworth’s best poems, are artists who lay line
or colour because they are themselves beautiful, not because
the design would be incomplete without them.   But Words-
worth at his best, with Shakespere and with Milton is
classic.

> ‘ No nightingale did ever chaunt
> More welcome notes to weary bands
> Of travellers, in some shady haunt,
> Among Arabian sands.
> No sweeter voice was ever heard,
> In spring time from the cuckoo-bird
> Breaking the silence of the seas
> Among the farthest Hebrides.’

What absolute purity, what simplicity, what directness,
and yet what music and felicity of utterance !
In his sonnets Wordsworth is at his best as artist.   The
sonnet was congenial to him because it was admirably suited
to his fashion of dealing with a single thought or single
wave of feeling.   He was accustomed to carry far into the
recesses of his mind one idea at a time, and there, free from
all interruption or invasion of other and foreign ideas, to
brood over it alone.   Thus closeted with himself, so to speak,
and with one all-absorbing object of thought, he saw it en-
tire, and expressed it in its loneliness and entirety.   The main
concept in his best sonnets unfolds itself with the organic
solitariness, the naturalness and beauty of a flower.   In
clearness of outline, in restrained grace, directness and purity

of expression, in a word, in the essentials of pure or classic art, they are perhaps the nearest of English poems to the Greek.

While still an undergraduate at Cambridge, Wordsworth visited France during a university vacation. The Revolution was in the air, and the young poet breathed that air with hopeful eagerness. The spectacle of a mighty nation preparing herself for a great leap towards freedom will stir the dullest heart. Wordsworth's heart was not idly stirred; but so kindled was the holy zeal for liberty in his breast, that in the following year he returned to bear a part in the cause of emancipation. Yet, though an ardent sympathiser, the iron heel of despotism had never pressed upon him, and he could not share in the lust for blood that inflamed the revolutionary populace. The September massacres dispelled the vision upon which his spirit had fed, the vision of a majestic moral victory. Wordsworth returned to England perplexed and saddened, and the years brought him a deeper reverence for the sober freedom of his own native land. By the death of a friend, Raisley Calvert, he became the possessor of a sum of money sufficient to enable him to give his whole strength to his beloved art, and in 1798 were published, in conjunction with Coleridge, the 'Lyrical Ballads,' The book, as we have seen, was an immediate failure, but with a certain grand indifference Wordsworth continued to write poetry. After a visit to Germany, he settled at Grasmere, in Westmoreland, now so famous as a place of pilgrimage for his worshippers, so well known

'Its one green island, and its winding shores,
The multitude of little rocky hills.'

Here Wordsworth developed his own peculiar method of

interpreting Nature. From his youth upwards he was more a deeply read in her lore than in books. In commenting on a couplet in one of his early poems—

> 'And fronting the bright west, the oak entwines
> Its darkening boughs and leaves in stronger lines,'

he said, 'This is feebly and imperfectly expressed, but I recollect distinctly the very spot where this first struck me. . . . The moment was important in my poetical history; for I date from it my consciousness of the infinite variety of natural appearances which had been unnoticed by the poets of any age or country, so far as I was acquainted with them, and made a resolution to supply in some degree the deficiency.' From the first, then, he was determined to be poet-laureate of the kingdom of Nature. But he did not end there; the kingdom of man claimed him also. Although he never lost the keen delight in every expression of her countenance in every variation of her moods, his sympathy with human nature widened and deepened. He came to view Nature in her relationship with man (a part of nature, but a unique part contemplating and rising above her), deriving her interest from human associations, and from the influences she breathes that mould and fashion the race. He was the first to show how potent these plastic influences were, with what subtlety and complexity they mingle with the latent elements of the individual character, and affect the life of heart and soul. He was not a painter of natural scenery, as other poets had and have been, but of its effects. In mere vivid description of beautiful, and especially of sublime natural phenomena, other poets have excelled him; but that was not the form of excellence he wished for. It is rather in his delineation, as John Stuart Mill said, 'of states of feeling, and of thought coloured by feeling, under the excitement of beauty,' that he is so distinctively original and powerful.

But if this were all, Wordsworth would not occupy the place he does in the hearts of the lovers of his poetry. Every original thinker sees and presents some new aspect of truth ; but to make all things new, to lead us to a point whence we survey familiar objects in relations unknown before, and which alter all our settled conceptions, to re-create the world in this way is the privilege of genius. This is what Wordsworth did. And so it is that in order to become a Wordsworthian, a citizen of this new-created world, one must in a sense be born again. Not in the hope that we shall become Wordsworthians, for perhaps it is better not to be a devotee at any one poetic shrine, but in the hope that where others have benefited we may also benefit, let us trace the more obvious lines of Words-worth's thought. Let us begin by saying that calling us aside from the strife and bustle of life, his poetry leads us to the cell of a solitary meditative student of Nature, endowed with a keener susceptibility than we for her sights and sounds, a kind of new sense for her loveliness and her teaching. But through the presentation of Nature in his poetry, as we have seen, runs a vein of quiet brooding thought. As the sun shines through and colours the stained window, so through the veil of sense upon which the natural scene is depicted shines the light of the poet's mind, suffusing and transforming it, making it a new thing for us. It is the same with the simplest incident he relates. With Wordsworth the world of outward things is a spur to reflection. The common objects on which he steadily keeps his eye develop an unthought-of significance. One by one, as he meditates on each, they yield up their secret, are presented in the setting of his impassioned contemplation, and become fresh sources of wisdom and of pleasure.

> ' The happy tone
> Of meditation slipping in between,
> The beauty coming, and the beauty gone.'

The familiar sights and sounds that daily greet eye and ear are transfigured by being lifted into a sphere above the physical, where they are no longer sights and sounds, but visions and whispers from an all-encircling spiritual universe

> ' He felt the sentiment of being spread
> O'er all that moves, and all that seemeth still ;
> The presences of Nature in the sky
> And on the earth ; the visions of the hills,
> And souls of lonely places.'   .

In the childhood of races, as of the individual, the universal frame of things is a source of unaffected wonder and joy ; the stars are great divine beings, the tree the haunt of the Dryad, the stream the dwelling place of the Nymph, the mountain the secret abode of the Oread. Something of the wonder and the mystery, the freshness and glory of things seen for the first time, Wordsworth reveals to us. As through the eyes of a child we look out upon the world, and see that it is inexpressibly fair ; we accept it with a child's heart, and people it with living guardian spirits. Not that he has created any Pantheon; the living spirit present in each living thing is not personified, but referred by Wordsworth to the central source of all life : in each blade of grass, in each bird among the leaves, in each mountain torrent, as well as in each human being, the presence of life is a proof of the presence of spirit, and thus from the

whole round world come voices to the soul of man, be-
cause it is in reality spirit that is in communion with spirit,
the spirit of man with the spirit of God.

> ' O glide, fair stream, for ever glide
>   Thy quiet soul on all bestowing,
>   Till all our minds for ever flow
>   As thy deep waters now are flowing.'

> ' It seems the eternal soul is clothed in thee,
>   With purer robes than those of flesh and blood,
>   And hath bestowed on thee a better good,
>   Unwearied joy, and life without its cares.'

If this be Pantheism, it is not a Pantheism of the schools.
Not at the moment only which is enriched by their presence,
are the sights and sounds of Nature precious to him. The
gathered experiences are stored in the mind, and ever
and anon the treasures of memory are brought forth.

If the note of the cuckoo, that wandering voice, has
once fallen upon his ear, it is with him for ever,—

> And I can listen to thee yet,
>   Can lie upon the plain
>   And listen, till I do beget
>   That golden time again.'

The song of the Highland maiden, as she reaps or binds
the grain, is an unforgettable melody,—

> 'The music in my heart I bore,
>   Long after it was heard no more.'

If a host of golden daffodils, tossing and twinkling along
the margin of the bay, has gladdened his eyes, it is a vision
of joy that no winter time can take away,—

> ' For oft when on my couch I lie,
>   In vacant or in pensive mood,
>   They flash upon that inward eye,
>   Which is the bliss of solitude ;
>   And then my heart with pleasure fills,
>   And dances with the daffodils.'

These 'treasured dreams of times long past,' are dwelt upon
in the poetry of Wordsworth with unfeigned pleasure, no
less real than that which accompanied the magic of the
first impression.

A supreme value of such a poet lies in the help he
renders towards the acquisition of a habit of thoughtfulness.
The bustle of constant occupation makes it difficult for us
to snatch a day or an hour for undisturbed meditation, for
quiet contemplation either of the eternal things around us,
or of our own hearts and minds.

> ' The world is too much with us ; late and soon,
>   Getting and spending we lay waste our powers.'

We are strangers to ourselves as well as strangers to
Nature, and our spiritual life is impoverished. Could we
spare, as Wordsworth would have us see to it that we
should spare, a part of our lives to the formation of a habit
of thoughtfulness, we might be awakened out of the tra-
ditional life we lead,—or rather acquiesce in, for it is not
really ours, but the life imposed upon us by the world of
social custom. Such a habit implanted would bear abund-
ant fruit in saner action and juster emotion. Wordsworth,
in his great ode on the 'Intimations of Immortality,' in a
way that to some minds appears a little fantastic, ascribes
to the child's view of the world a deeper significance than
to that of the man. He believed that the child, new come
from his divine home, was the best guide to truth, that he

looked out upon Nature with eyes undimmed by 'the film of familiarity,' and saw further than the sagest of thinkers

'Into the eternal deep
Haunted for ever by the eternal mind.'

In this poem, magnificent as it is, we have an approach to that definiteness of schematic thought which always proved fatal to Wordsworth's poetry as poetry. The phrase, 'at his best' has often to be used concerning him ; and it has a special force, because the poet and the philosopher were not fused in him, because he is often merely philosophising when he believed himself to be writing poetry, and, having at any time set himself a poetic task, he carries it through doggedly, without previous enquiry at the oracle whether the gods were favourable or not. We seem, as Russell Lowell wittily said, to 'recognise two voices in him, as Stephano did in Caliban. There are Jeremiah and his scribe Baruch. If the prophet cease from dictating, the amanuensis, rather than be idle, employs his pen in jotting down some anecdotes of his master—how he one day went out and saw an old woman, and the next day did not, and so came home and dictated some verses on this ominous phenomenon, and how another day he saw a cow! These marginal annotations have been carelessly taken up into the text, have been religiously held by the pious to be ortho- dox scripture, and by dexterous exegesis have been made to yield deeply oracular meanings. Presently the real prophet takes up the word again, and speaks as one divinely in- spired, the voice of a higher and invisible power.' It is unnecessary to illustrate the work of these two Wordsworths. They are so unlike that one has difficulty in recognising any relationship between them at all. Take this as a statement of facts, which might serve as an introduction in prose to a poem to follow :—

> 'Once in a lonely hamlet I sojourned,
> In which a lady driven from France did dwell;
> The big and lesser griefs with which she mourned
> In friendship she to me would often tell.'

This is Wordsworth the scribe, who has left many such samples of his hand. Who could believe that he is related to the author of this, for instance :—

> 'She shall be sportive as the fawn
> That, wild with glee, across the lawn
> Or up the mountain springs;
> And hers shall be the breathing balm,
> And hers the silence and the calm
> Of mute insensate things.
>
> The floating clouds their state shall lend
> To her; for her the willow bend;
> Nor shall she fail to see,
> E'en in the motions of the storm,
> Grace that shall mould the maiden's form
> By silent sympathy.
>
> The stars of midnight shall be dear
> To her; and she shall lean her ear
> In many a secret place,
> Where rivulets dance their wayward round,
> And beauty born of murmuring sound
> Shall pass into her face.'

'It is becoming and decorous,' to quote again from Landor, 'that due honours be paid to Wordsworth; undue have injured him. Discriminating praise, mingled with calm censure, is more beneficial than lavish praise without it.' Those who have at heart a capacity for true reverence will shrink from its bestowal where it is not truly merited. It is because undue honours are injurious, not less to him who gives than to him who receives, that we must be careful of our praise as well as of our blame.

Unlike Milton or Goethe or Tennyson, Wordsworth was not a conscious artist, or more truly, perhaps, he was greatest when he was least conscious of how his effects were attained. He would have treated with impatience any suggestion that tended to set execution in poetry in higher place than its matter, any criticism which spoke of it as primarily an art. 'Every great poet is a teacher,' he said; 'I wish to be considered as a teacher or as nothing.' A dangerous doctrine when so strenuously urged by a poet himself! In his anxiety to teach, just as in his anxiety to be true to Nature, he forgot at times his allegiance to his Muse. He forgot that a point cannot be pressed or returned upon as in oratory, that poetry is not concerned with the statement of facts, and that the effect must be immediate or it is not obtained at all. The business of prose is to expand, to detail, to analyse, to press home by repetition. 'Poetry,' as Bagehot said, 'must be memorable and emphatic, intense, and soon over.' It is indeed permissible, in a long poem, to relax at times the strain; the wave of thought and feeling may rise and fall, but throughout the motion must be apparent; a motionless surface argues stagnation. Wordsworth had no power of dealing with action, no faculty for the rapid development of scene and incident. His figures are statuesque and solitary, like the leech-gatherer,—

'Motionless as a cloud the old man stood.'

When we come to read the longer poems, we find yet other limitations of his genius. It would be impossible for any man to have less sense of humour, and with Words worth it 'was even a frightful *minus* quantity.' What a cramping limitation is that! Then the longer poems are *structureless*. He does not seem to have been capable of handling any but detached emotions, and these only in their simplest elements, and arising out of the simplest relationships of life; the affections of a man for friends, for wife or children, his feelings in the presence of the most universal sources of feeling, fear, joy, love and death. A subject that, in its poetic treatment demands scheme, proportional development, in a word, poetic architectonics, was beyond his strength, or rather did not lie within the verge of his own special demesne. While then the 'Excursion' and the 'Prelude' contain fine meditative passages, rich in noble and affecting thought, the transcripts of his own spiritual broodings, they are very far from being essential poetry. When it becomes possible to pick out passages or lines from a poem which suffer no loss from the absence of the context, or, as in the case of some of Wordsworth's longer poems, with the positive gain to the reader of a feeling of relief, such a work may be set down at once among the mass of unsuccessful poetry, of poetry that has fallen short of the excellence at which it aimed. For, as has already been said, it is not in the massing of details that the poet's province lies, but in leaving upon his reader's mind one pure simple affecting outline, one undying image of perfect feature. The Muse is not easily won over to extend her favour so far as to preside over the production of an epic or philosophic poem of a dozen books. Once or twice in the history of the world to a highly honoured son she has permitted the successful achievement of such a task, but only once or twice. Many whom she has favoured with an occasional smile, have too hastily presumed upon her con-

stancy of kindness, and have embarked upon enterprises for
which they had neither native strength nor heavenly man-
date.   A philosophical teacher Wordsworth aspired to
be, and a philosophical teacher he was, but his philosophi-
cal doctrines are not the source of his greatness.   When
he introduces a definite moral or spiritual precept into
his verse, the poetry loses, and we are little the better of
the precept.   But, fortunately, at times when he was un-
conscious of it, the lady of poesy, instead of her sister of
philosophy, stood by his side, and at these times—

> ' From worlds not quickened by the sun
> A portion of his gift is won ;
> An intermingling of heaven's pomp is shed
> On ground that British shepherds tread.'

Wordsworth's life was self-centred.   He was far from perfect
as a man as he was far from perfect as a poet.   A solitary
from his youth, living apart from men, communing with his
own heart, and with the world of Nature as his chief com-
panion, caring little to extend his horizon, the narrowness
and egotism which forced him to an over-estimate of the
worth of his own observations and reflections were inevit-
able ; and these, too, were probably the reasons why he was
no sure critic of his own poetry.   But while not a sure
critic of it, he often struck on the point of its chief excel-
lence.   As Emerson tells us, ' He preferred such of his
poems as touched the affections to any others ; for whatever
is didactic,—what theories of society, and so on, might
perish quickly ; but whatever combined a truth with an
affection was good to-day and good for ever.'   How admir-
able this is !   Dealing with the simple affections, with the
hopes and fears that are common to all, with the duties
that all have imposed upon them, dealing with these as they

appear among plain country folk, withdrawn from the
feverish and hurried life of cities and their societies
dominated by ephemeral fashions and empty displays, here
Wordsworth shines, and will continue to shine. Whatever
is in him of calculated didacticism, of theories of society,
will, no doubt, as he anticipated, decay ; but because he has
so marvellously combined truths with affections, he is good
to-day and good for ever. Wordsworth's mission seems to
have been, above all, to find joys and consolations for the
spirit of man where they had lain unsuspected. It was his
good fortune to discover 'a joy in widest commonalty
spread,' and to make known 'the soothing thoughts that
spring out of human suffering.' A poet who can do this,
who can thus turn man's extremity to glorious gain, will
remain humanity's noble and puissant friend. We have
seen that he had weaknesses, personal faults as well as
poetical, but we may pass lightly over the shortcomings of
so great a benefactor. There is no genius so all-embracing
as to be without limitations, and we do well in thinking of
a great man's failure to reach perfection as a mere mark of
his humanity. It has been said that his poetry lacks fire
and passion. Fire and passion are not to be expected in
the poetry of a man of meditative cast ; its qualities are of
another, and perhaps a rarer order. As Arnold wrote :—

> ' Time may restore us in his course
> Goethe's sage mind and Byron's force ;
> But when will Europe's later hour
> Again find Wordsworth's healing power ? '

And yet does not at times an unlooked-for flash reveal the
presence of an inspiring force beneath the quiet surface of
his mind?   '.

> ' Armour rusting in his halls
>   On the blood of Clifford calls :—
>   " Quell the Scot," exclaims the Lance—
>   Bear me to the heart of France,
>   Is the longing of the shield.'

We must not too hastily conclude that so great a man and poet was lacking in any of the essentials of exalted manhood or of true poetry. And here surely is passion in a sonnet addressed to Toussant l'Ouverture—passion generous and splendid,—

> ' Though fallen thyself, never to rise again,
>   Live and take comfort. Thou hast left behind
>   Powers that will work for thee ; air, earth and skies ;
>   There's not a breathing of the common wind
>   That will forget thee ; thou hast great allies ;
>   Thy friends are exultations, agonies
>   And love, and man's unconquerable mind.'

Wordsworth's gift to his race lies in his awakening power, disclosing to us undreamt - of and inexhaustible sources of pure pleasures and unfailing consolations to which we are blinded by devotion to the things of the passing hour,—in this awakening power, and in his power of increasing our love and reverence for humanity in its humblest place or estate of fortune, by withdrawing our attention from the objects of every-day ambition, and fixing it upon the destiny and the feelings we share with all our fellows of like mortal lineage. Throughout his poetry, his unswerving loyalty to whatsoever things are just and lovely, and of good report, gives us fresh confidence in life. No poet has shown so triumphantly how strong in its barest simplicity may be that poetry, whose theme is

> ' No other than the very heart of man.'

CHAPTER V

NEO-CLASSICISM

Keats—Landor—Leigh Hunt

THE human mind, in the effort to give artistic expression
to its multiform life, has pursued two broadly differing
methods, each having its root in a soil of moral, intellectual,
spiritual and social conditions foreign to the other. The
one method is governed by a determination to attempt
artistic expression of that alone which is seen and grasped
in its entirety; the other is mastered by the desire to
suggest outlying truths not yet wholly brought into the
region of clearly-defined knowledge. The characteristics
of the first, precision of idea, singleness of emotional
motive, simplicity of form, are best exhibited in the Greek
drama. Those of the second, suggestiveness in thought,
complexity in its presentment, are most easily accessible to
the student in the Elizabethan or Shakesperian drama.
The forms of the Greek faith, the conceptions of the gods
and goddesses of Olympus, were the result of an endeavour,
in answer to a pressing intellectual need, to reduce to
harmony the visible and invisible powers at work in the
universe. The Greek artists, while they clearly recognised
that a valid and final explanation of Nature and man was

not here offered, were content to acquiesce in the popular cosmogony as affording the only possible basis for art at all. The mediæval artist, by reason of the entrance through Christianity into this life of a revelation connecting it with a vast scheme, a revelation involving truths beyond precise comprehension, was carried into dealing with imperfectly ascertained knowledge, with human life as encircled by mystery, with the ' something from beyond his present being.' The Middle Ages painted man's destiny on earth in sombre colours, exalting by comparison the unstained light of heaven which it was man's privilege and duty to attain. In the hour of his trial and of his weakness, Christianity held out to him the promise of a divine assistance. His weakness was his only plea, and revelation the pledge of a heavenly home. Without a future to which he could thus flee for refuge in the season of affliction, forced back upon himself, the Greek exalted the life of untroubled Stoic or Epicurean acceptance of the gifts of fortune, of evil as of good. The dignity of man was thus accentuated, in contradistinction to his sin and frailty which were the key to the mediæval economy of life. While then Greek art brought into necessary prominence the consolations open to the spirit in the eternal shapes of beauty offered in Nature to be enjoyed as long as life lasted, and left in the background the unexplored because inaccessible provinces of ultimate truths which served no end in art, Christian artists, because an opening had been made into that hitherto untravelled world, dwelt upon the glories that eye had not seen nor ear heard, and their art was the product of imagination conscious of an eternal life and abiding spiritual presences on earth.

The classic spirit in art is for ever associated with form

and calm and order ; the mediæval with colour, enthusiasm and mystery: for the one believed in the senses, and fed them with beauty, keeping as its ideal, 'self-reverence, self-knowledge, self-control;' the other discredited the earthly senses, and starved them, and had for its ideal, self-abandonment, a knowledge of God, and spiritual rapture. Approaching truth by analysis, Greek art draws in outline and speaks a direct language ; approaching truth by intuition and faith, Christian art paints in colour, and speaks in symbol. The Greek, like Sophocles, believed in the real world with all its certainties. He saw all that he did see with unfailing clearness of vision ; and the spirit of precision and simplicity bears rule in the sphere of his artistic creation. The Christian of the Middle Ages, like Dante, believed in an invisible world, with all its splendours and glories seen only by the eye of the soul ; and inspired fervour, emotional glow, are the marks of his art. The light streaming from that other world transforms and irradiates this. Christian morality was a morality of personal devotion to a Divine Master, informed by the passionate desire for a harmony with the will of God, according to the law of love. In it the emotional element dominated the merely intellectual. Classic morality, at its highest point, with the Greek and Roman philosophers, was a morality of adherence to an impersonal law, a high resolve of the intellect to live in harmony with the order of the Kosmos, or, in the well-known phrase—'according to Nature.' Each attitude of mind due to its surrounding conditions had noble qualities of its own ; and to the artistic expression of each belonged, as has been suggested, the noble qualities natural and proper to itself.

We are accustomed to call all great art classic, since the

qualities of repose, symmetry, and simplicity, possessed by the best Greek art, are qualities indispensable to high artistic creation, whatever others may be added to them.   Thus Dante and Shakespere are classic, because, though they deal with vastly more complicated issues than Sophocles or Euripides allowed themselves, and permit their imaginations to push out into an ocean of mystery over which the Greek poets never voyaged, in spite of this, their poetical creation has the sharpness of outline, both in idea and language, of classic poetry dealing with much simpler issues. In the main conceptions, and in the details, of Dante and Shakespere, there are added to sharpness of outline, a passion and a depth, a glow of heat and colour, and a suggestiveness, for which it will be vain to look in any Greek writer.   Thus Shakespere and Dante, and, indeed, all modern artists of the very first class, are both classic and romantic.   They have the clear-cut serenity, the bareness of idea, the precision, the directness of appeal, such as is made by a statue by Phidias, with the wider range, the richness and the fervour of a painting by Raphael or Michael Angelo.   In English literature, Milton is the great classic : not that he is unversed in the changed aspects of all human problems due to Christianity, but because he had imbibed the spirit of Greek art by long and close acquaintanceship with its best products.   He is classic by his self-possession and by the simplicity of his motives, by the avoidance, in his character-drawing, of any lines save of outline delineation, by the clearness of his main scheme, and the subordination of parts to the whole, and by the sure, sustained dignity of his metrical movement.   Milton closes one and opens another era.   When we come to the so-called Augustan age of English literature, to the so-called classical writers, Dryden

and Pope and Johnson, we find it classical in a sense, but
not in the real sense. Dryden and Pope and Johnson
possess the qualities of simplicity, repose, precision ; but
they are simple because they deal only with the surface-facts
of life, calm because they have never known in themselves
what it is to be profoundly moved, precise because they
merely repeat in terser phrase the current opinions of the
time. Simplicity, repose, precision, are only admirable and
precious when threatened by imaginative wealth, emotional
fervour, intellectual profundity—only admirable when pre-
served in spite of and amidst these splendid dangers. Pope
and his followers were in perfect security from these dangers ;
and the classic qualities of their verse, therefore, nominal
rather than real, cannot be rated high. The reaction against
this pseudo-classicism had set in before Keats' bright star
rose above the literary horizon ; but it was left for him to
break more utterly away from the traditions of the poetic
method so long supreme than any other English poet, save,
perhaps, Landor, born twenty years before him, and whose
first volume was published in the year in which Keats was
born. Keats' genius was not nourished upon contemporary
literature. His first inspiration, like his poetic awakening,
was due to Spenser and the 'Faery Queen.' The Eliza-
bethans, not the men of Queen Anne's reign, were his an-
cestors. At school he was remarkable chiefly for his com-
bative spirit, his delight in battle ; but when Spenser's
glorious planet swam into his ken, his destiny was deter-
mined—from that hour poetry was supreme with him, he
was pure poet. ' Had there been no such thing as literature,
Keats would have dwindled into a cypher,' said De Quincey ;
but the record of his early life proves him to have been no
sentimental girl, whose day-dreams are her most serious

occupation. At school he cared little for books, and was the leader in war. At fifteen years of age the tide turned, and he became a voracious reader; but, had there been no such thing as literature, he would probably have chosen a military life, and achieved distinction therein. It is not surprising that Spenser should have so fastened upon his imagination. 'The Poets' Poet,' with his magnificent superfluity of graces, his luxuriance of language and of melody, his splendours of colour, his seriousness of purpose intermingled with the magic thread of romance, fascinates, and will continue to fascinate, all imaginative minds. Keats was taken captive, Spenser's golden chain was riveted upon his wrist, and though at basis his genius was of Hellenic stamp, he was made willing bondman in the service of romanticism. Undisciplined as all Elizabethan poetry is, as compared with ancient models, Spenser is chief offender, the most undisciplined of all. The 'Faery Queen' is a poetic wilderness, a place of true enchantment; but a wilderness in which we easily lose our way, though without regret. Keats' early manner is the manner of Spenser; but it was not there that his real mastery lay. There meet in him the Renaissance feeling for beauty, the Hellenic delight in perfect form, and the new passion for Nature lately entered into the sphere of the poet. We find in him all these elements; but there can be little doubt that, as 'Hyperion' shows, the bent of mind towards simplicity would have in the end predominated, had he attained poetic maturity. The various elements are all present in him, but when he speaks in his most mature tone, it is the accent of Sophocles, not the accent of Spenser, we hear

'The moving waters at their priest-like task
Of pure ablution round earth's human shores.'

'Like anxious men
Who on wide plains gather in panting troops,
When earthquakes jar their battlements and towers.'

'By her in stature the tall Amazon
Had stood a pigmy's height ; she would have ta'en
Achilles by the hair and bent his neck ;
Or with a finger stayed Ixion's wheel.'

Here is no trace of Spenser's prodigal opulence, here in
his maturity he is Greek. And, indeed, Keats has no vital
relationship with Spenser, who, in spite of the purple splen-
dour and regal embroidery of his singing robes, was at heart
a grave Puritan, ' our sage and serious poet,' as Milton said,
' whom I dare be known to think a better teacher than
Scotus or Aquinas.' In his youth Keats was intoxicated
by Spenser's beauty of face and person, not by the inner
graces of his character ; and though he was so profoundly
influenced as to model his own manner upon that of Spenser,
when he grew to be his own master and the ruler of his own
house, his method is his own, and in accent he is next-of-
kin to the reigning poet-kings. As he grew in years he grew
in mastery of his art. Gradually he came to prize the
impression of the whole design above the parts that com-
prise it, to have constantly before his eye, even when
elaborating a subsidiary curve, the imperious idea that
controlled all and was subserved by all. Free and sweeping
as the lines of a great artist are, they are under the restraining
guidance of the central conception ; he permits no ornament
for the sake of ornament, no meaningless arabesque, but
preserves the essential unity, as it is preserved in ' Macbeth '
or ' King Lear,' amid the utmost multiplicity of detail. At
the stage in which he wrote ' Endymion,' Keats had the
youthful view of poetry, that it should be rarely prodigal of

beauties. ' I think poetry should surprise by a fine excess,'
he said. The sentence conveys the very essence of the
Romantic spirit, that it should surprise by a fine excess ;
whereas the very essence of the classic spirit is that it
should elevate and purify rather than surprise, and that
through a noble reserve, a grandeur of frugality. But his
poetic ideals changed, and Keats' conception of what poetry
ought to be, came to be juster and fuller than those left us
by any other poet. The stage at which he cried, ' Oh, for a
life of sensations rather than of thought,' was passing, had
indeed passed away before his death, and he was devoting
himself to ' the ardours rather than the pleasures of song.'
' Let us never forget,' as his biographer, Lord Houghton,
said, ' that, wonderful as are the poems of Keats, yet, after
all, they are rather the records of a poetical education than
the accomplished work of a mature artist.' What should we
have known of Sophocles, of Dante, of Shakespere, of
Milton, had they died each at the age of twenty-four ? The
verbal, musical and emotional richness of his poetry is
admittedly out of all proportion to its intellectual power, and
even more out of proportion to its moral or spiritual inten-
tion. But we do not look for the furthest reaches of art in
its earliest beginnings. Keats began where Shakespere
began. Before ' Hamlet ' and ' Macbeth ' and ' Lear ' there
were other and lesser achievements ; and before drama was
attempted at all came the youthful genius-prompted exuber-
ances of melody and colour and passion in ' Venus and
Adonis ' and the ' Rape of Lucrece.' The poet whose
dreams were of the order which he thus describes in a letter,
we need have no critical diffidence in regarding as the poet
of by far the greatest promise in England since Shakespere
himself :—

'I feel more and more every day, as my imagination strengthens, that I do not live in this world alone, but in a thousand worlds. No sooner am I alone than shapes of epic greatness are stationed around me, and serve my spirit the office which is equivalent to a King's Bodyguard : "then tragedy with sceptred pall comes sweeping by." According to my state of mind, I am with Achilles shouting in the trenches, or with Theocritus in the vales of Sicily ; or throw my whole being into Troilus, and repeating those lines, "I wander like a lost soul upon the Stygian bank, staying for waftage," I melt into the air with a voluptuousness so delicate that I am content to be alone.'

If Keats could write with the light magic of a touch such as is displayed here, for example, in 'Endymion':—

> 'Whence came ye, merry damsels ! whence came ye !
> So many, and so many, and such glee?
> Why have ye left your bowers desolate,
>   Your lutes and gentler fate ?
> We follow Bacchus ! Bacchus on the wing,
>   A conquering !
> Bacchus, young Bacchus ! good or ill betide,
> We dance before him thorough kingdoms wide :—
> Come hither, lady fair, and joined be
>   To our wild minstrelsy !'

If he could write like this, he could reach a higher strain, not far from the very highest, reached only when the supreme vision is vouchsafed—he could reach the truth, the gravity and the loveliness of this, when, speaking of melancholy, he says :—

> 'She dwells with Beauty—Beauty that must die :
>   And Joy, whose hand is ever at his lips
> Bidding adieu ; and aching Pleasure nigh
>   Turning to poison while the bee-mouth sips :

Ay, in the very temple of Delight
Veil'd Melancholy has her sovran shrine,
Though seen of none save him whose strenuous tongue
Can burst Joy's grape against his palate fine :
His soul shall taste the sadness of her might,
And be among her cloudy trophies hung.'

We have seen that Keats shared in the new feeling for Nature. Nature, for her own sake, had never before the close of the 18th century so occupied the minds of the poets. Keats' nature-painting is not the mere detailed description of Thomson or of Cowper, it is rather Chaucer's enriched. There is the same freshness of apprehension and of touch as in Chaucer, for, like Chaucer, his contact with Nature was direct. Those pictures of Nature are not likest her which reproduce with photographic accuracy her every detail, but which, with the fewest strokes, convey to the eye of the mind an impression of the whole as received by the poet himself. In seeing and representing the features which are characteristic, the lines wherein the true expression lies, in this is the difficulty only overcome by genius. Keats' feeling for Nature was rich and full ; his was the seeing eye and the understanding heart; and thrilled as he was by the subtle effluences of her beauty—' I have loved the principle of beauty in all things,' he said—he had the gift of recording his emotion in the key of words appropriate and perfect. Is not this the key of Nature's music at the close of a day of opening summer ?

' I cannot see what flowers are at my feet,
Nor what soft incense hangs upon the boughs,
But, in embalmed darkness, guess each sweet
Wherewith the seasonable month endows
The grass, the thicket, and the fruit-tree wild,
White hawthorn and the pastoral eglantine,

Fast fading violets cover'd up in leaves,
And mid-May's eldest child,
The coming musk-rose, full of dewy wine,
The murmurous haunt of flies on summer eves.'

Magical as many of his effects are, Mr Palgrave is right in noting that his landscape falls short of the landscape of Shelley in its comparative absence of the larger features of sky and earth; it is in foreground work that he excels: while again, in comparison with Wordsworth, Keats rests satisfied with exquisitely true delineation, and has little thought of allying Nature with human sympathy; still less of penetrating and rendering her deeper eternal significance.

On the life as on the poetry of Keats a potent influence was the friendship of Leigh Hunt. The author of 'Rimini' was a lover of Spenser and of the Italians who were Spenser's models. Although, as editor of the *Examiner*, he was a prominent soldier in the cause of Liberalism, and suffered for his faith and courage, he never lost a native light-heartedness and gaiety which gave a winning charm to his character and person. Kindred poetic tastes and mutual admiration (deepest at first, of course, on the side of Keats, for Leigh Hunt was already at the beginning of the friendship a poet of reputation) drew these two men very closely together. The motto most appropriate to the title-page of Leigh Hunt's poetical works would be that sentence of Oliver Goldsmith's which so well characterises the motive of his own gentle art—' Innocently to amuse the imagination in this dream of life is wisdom.' Leigh Hunt does not permit the 'Sturm und Drang' of life to appear in his verse; he kept far, far off the insidious, unintelligible world, and loved to lose himself in the enchanted forests of the

H

chivalric epics of Italy.   To Keats his kindness was that of
a tender, admiring and unfailing friend, and only in the in-
fluence of his somewhat too luscious and conversationally
easy style was he anything but a true helper and guide to
the younger poet.   At Leigh Hunt's house Keats met
Shelley, with whom, however, he was never intimate, and
Haydon, the painter, who became his friend.

To the influence of Spenser and of Leigh Hunt we may
trace the mannerisms of Keats and his liberties with the
language which drew from De Quincey the characteristic
remark that ' he had trampled upon his mother tongue as
with the hoofs of a buffalo.'   The laxities occur, however,
only in the early longer poems ; in the lyrics, and as he
grew older, they are not to be found.   Here, however, we
strike on one of the essential differences between Keats
and that other English poet who was a Roman at heart and
a Greek at brain—Landor.   ' I hate false words,' wrote the
latter, 'and seek with care, difficulty and moroseness those
that fit the thing.'   From the first the intention of Landor's
art was evident--fully realised, clear-cut ideas, and words
that fit the thing.   He lived aloof not only from his own
time, but from modern life and thought altogether.   He is
freer from all trace of the romantic spirit, freer, perhaps,
than was even Milton, and his charm is the charm of noble
severity.   Landor's indifference to Spenser—

> ' Thee, gentle Spenser fondly led,*
> But me he mostly sent to bed '—

serves as clue to the wide diversity between himself and
Keats in poetic apprehension, and in the modes and aims
of their common art, though both were poets upon whose

* To Wordsworth,

imaginations had powerfully seized the marvellous concep-
tions of the mythology of Greece, and who had recognised
its essential and unique poetic value by finding in it the
most congenial themes. The influences of the classical
renaissance of the fifteenth century reached England to-
gether with the spirit of Italian romance ; and in Spenser
we have Aristotelian scheme, Italian mysticism and colour,
and the old Celtic legends, in bewildering but fascinating
confusion. No poet, after his time, could avoid taking in
with his breath each constituent element of the atmosphere
thus composed so completely as to give to his workman-
ship the distinctive stamp of purely romantic, much less of
purely classic, art. The spell that Spenser, and, later, the
Greek myths, threw over Keats, proving the susceptibility
of his nature, as he said, ' to the principle of beauty in all
. things,' was the spell that determined the aim and tendency
of his art. His treatment of the subjects taken from the
mythology of Greece is essentially—and here he is distin-
guished from Landor—in the opulent romantic vein; and even
' Hyperion,' with its unique grandeur, though, as we have
seen, in diction nearer Sophocles than Spenser, or, at least,
nearing him, is rather a *tour de force* in an antique mode
than a natural artistic product. Though in Virgil and
Milton we have splendid exceptions, it may truly be said
that the greatest poetry of the world drew its inspiration
from the times which gave it birth. A revived interest, a
recollected passion, can have little inspiring force beside the
glow of a present enthusiasm, the rapture of a living love.
From Keats we date the English poetry of culture, the
poetry which depends for its effect upon sentiments that
bore their fruit in past ages, upon the glories of ancient
heroisms, the pathos of dead faiths, the romance of buried

loves—which is distinguished by its subtle blending with the feelings of to-day of all that appeals to the sense for beauty in the history of the human race, and comes to us fraught with the indescribable power over the emotions that belongs to perfections and ideals that are dead, that can never more be revived or become ours. From Keats we may date the stream of culture-poetry, distinguished by its beauty rather than by its strength, by its music and delicate curve rather than by its swiftness and volume. In classic poetry, including under the term the highest poetry of all ages, action and character are predominant; in romantic, especially in the hands of the weaker artists, sentiment is paramount, action and character are displaced and neglected. And it is here Landor fails to reach the true classic elevation; sentiment overpowers action in 'Gebir,' for example, as it was never permitted to do even by Euripides, who was condemned by the critics for his degradation of tragedy in this very respect. With Keats sentiment is supreme; he was too young to have learnt the management of action, too ignorant of the world to penetrate character. Landor, who was from the first a follower in the footsteps of the Attic tragedians, drew even in 'Gebir,' written when he was but twenty years old, his portraits with a firm hand; but was to the last deficient in the power that sets forth one simple, grand, entire action, which, when the details are forgotten, stands out sharply outlined against the mental horizon. Such is the action of the 'Œdipus,' of 'Macbeth,' of 'Paradise Lost.' It must be remembered that the Attic dramatists found such actions ready to hand in the traditions of early Greek history; Shakespere, in early British legends, some of which had been previously dramatised, and in the heroic records of the early English kings, when kingship meant personal rule. Greek and English drama were written, too, at a time when heroic action such as was dealt with in tragedy did not belong to and loom out of a misty past, but was understood and realised as a part of the living present. The interest of the poet in his *dramatis personæ* was near and vital; and without such near and vital interest in the action and character treated of, great dramatic achievement is impossible. Milton, by a supreme effort of imagination, aided by his Hebrew spirit, which brought him close to the persons and time of his plot, created in large measure his own history; but no poet since his day has so thoroughly realised a period involving action suitable to drama or epic as to make them really great or vital. Goethe is not great in his 'Iphigenia,' but in his 'Faust,' the embodiment of the whole world of modern ideas—in his representation of a unity of thought comparable to, and taking the place of, the grand unity of action which marks Attic and Elizabethan tragedy. We do not read Keats because he was the bearer of any noble message to his age, and therefore to all ages to come—because he was a herald of divine tidings; he was not such a herald. We read him for his amazing felicity of phrase, for his magical melodies, for his sensuous, romantic imagination; and we mingle a reverence with our admiration, because we feel that his maturity, had he reached it, might have rivalled Milton's in sublimity. Landor we read —those of us who do read him—for quite other reasons. Not, indeed, that that 'grand old Pagan,' as Carlyle called him, had any portion of the prophetic fire that Keats lacked. He, too, lived in retirement from his own age, lived in secluded communion with the best periods of Greek and Roman civilisation, caring little for any English writers except Shakespere and Milton, and without reverence for the other names of the great dramatic epoch of our literature. Keats' catholicity of appreciation widened his intellectual world; it was wider than Landor's, although Landor was scholar enough to be able to divide his allegiance, deep and true as it was to both, between Athens and Rome. The peculiar limitation of mind that made Landor essentially a Greek, and that in a far truer sense than Keats, or even Milton, is displayed in every department of his work: in his distaste for Spenser, in his depreciation of the Elizabethan dramatists, in his contempt for Goethe, in his utter aloofness from the world of modern ideas. Take this as typical of his own mind, put into the mouth of Boccaccio:—'What is there lovely in poetry unless there be moderation and composure? Are they not better than the hot, uncontrollable harlotry of a flaunting, dishevelled enthusiasm? Whoever has the power of creating, has likewise the inferior power of keeping his creations in order. The best poets are the most impressive, because their steps are regular; for without regularity there is neither strength nor state. Look at Sophocles, look at Æschylus, look at Homer.' Or this, spoken by Aspasia, to the same purpose:—'Poetry has not only her days of festival, but also her days of abstinence, and, unless upon some that are set apart, prefers the graces of sedateness to the revelry of enthusiasm.' For one who possesses by nature, or has acquired, the keen intellectual relish for the austerer grandeurs, the graver beauties of poetry, Landor's severe dignity will never cease to charm; and upon many it may have the effect of making the high tones of romantic colourists seem tawdry and offensive by comparison. And yet, it may be asked, where is there in 'Gebir' or 'Count Julian' a passage like that in 'Hyperion' which describes the portents in the Palace of the Sun, portents that threaten divine dynasty itself?

> ' Not at dog's howl or gloom-bird's hated screech,
> Or the familiar visiting of one
> Upon the first toll of his passing-bell,
> Or prophesyings of the midnight lamp ;
> But horrors portion'd to a giant nerve
> Oft made Hyperion ache. His palace bright,
> Bastion'd with pyramids of glowing gold,
> And touched with shade of bronzed obelisks,
> Glar'd a blood-red through all its thousand courts,
> Arches, and domes, and fiery galleries ;
> And all its curtains of Aurorian clouds
> Flush'd angrily ; while sometimes eagle's wings,
> Unseen before by gods or wondering men,
> Darken'd the place ; and neighing steeds were heard,
> Not heard before by gods or wondering men.
> Also, when he would taste the spicy wreaths
> Of incense breath'd aloft from sacred hills,
> Instead of sweets, his ample palate took
> Savour of poisonous brass and metal sick.'

Perhaps there is nothing in Landor quite like this, where classicism and romanticism meet ; but at times his voice falls upon the ear with a quiet solemnity, sweetness and fulness of intonation that, once heard, can never be forgotten.

> ' Artemidora ! Gods invisible,
> While thou art lying faint along the couch,
> Have tied the sandal to thy slender feet,
> And stand beside thee, ready to convey
> Thy weary steps where other rivers flow,
> Refreshing shades will waft thy weariness
> Away, and voices like thy own come near
> And nearer, and solicit an embrace.'

That a poet with this truly Olympian manner should want

readers is not a little surprising, until we recollect how popular judgments are arrived at. De Quincey tells us that to 'Gebir' belonged, for some time, the sublime distinction of having enjoyed only two readers, those two being Southey and himself. Not knowing Southey at the time, 'I vainly conceited myself,' he writes, 'to be the one sole purchaser and reader of this poem.' Whatever may have been the truth of this, 'Gebir,' as well as Landor's other poems, have had many and worthy readers since De Quincey. His circle, indeed, will never be large, but at no time will it be other than deeply appreciative, and that with absolute sincerity.

Landor's word for his time was not a moral or a spiritual word; it was like the poetry of Keats, a plea for beauty. Landor's pleadings for beauty were the more majestic, Keats' the more impassioned; Landor's rather for the pure beauty of perfect form, Keats' for warm loveliness of rich and glowing colour; the one was a pleader for beauty that is seen, the other for beauty that is felt.

Landor, it must be confessed, made a nearer approach to that highest reach of art where it stimulates or consoles the spirit of man.

> 'I strove with none, for none was worth my strife;
> Nature I loved, and, next to Nature, art;
> I warmed both hands before the fire of life;
> It sinks, and I am ready to depart.'

Nevertheless, he was, as Emerson said, a man full of thoughts rather than a man of ideas. He was not a revealer, but an artist, who drew his materials from the inexhaustible quarries of heroic history, and shaped his statues after the models of the ancient craftsmen. Nor is he a sure guide in any department of man's mental activity. His personality was too knotted and gnarled by temper and prejudice to preserve a constant lucidity and sanity with its strength. It is impossible to feel a perfect confidence in him; we may enjoy to the uttermost, but we cannot trust to the uttermost. Although no priest of a new transforming or vivifying faith, although contemplative rather than animating or fortifying, Landor tends towards culture, towards that widening of sympathy, and especially towards that refining of feeling in which culture consists; and, to quote again from Emerson, he is 'a sure resource in solitude.'

But when we speak of him as a sure resource in solitude, it is not as poet only. Even when treating exclusively of poetry, it would be unwarrantable to omit all reference to his prose. If there be any excuse for the use of the phrase 'a prose poet,' Landor affords it. 'Good prose,' he makes Marvel say in one of his conversations, 'to say nothing of the original thoughts it conveys, may be infinitely varied in modulation. It is only an extension of metres, an amplification of harmonies, of which even the best and most varied poetry admits but few.' With him as with Coleridge, poetry was the refuge from the cares and distractions of the outward world; it was, he tells us, his amusement, prose his study and business. And we may so far credit his own judgment as to look in his prose work for a complete history of his mind. 'Do you think,' Carlyle wrote of one of his dialogues, 'the grand old Pagan wrote that piece just now? The sound of it is like the ring of Roman swords upon the helmets of barbarians. An unsubduable old Roman!' An unsubduable old Roman he was, as the story of his life clearly demonstrates; after reading which one wonders how such irascible temper could live with such pure tenderness of heart. Landor's prose style is formed on Latin

models, and has the stately regularity, the impressive march
of the periods of Cicero; but with its measured cadence
mingles at times an almost bird-like note of appealing soft-
ness, which we do not look for, or look for elsewhere in
vain, outside the realm of poetry.   Strength without parade,
purity without affectation, precision without loss of grace;
these he attained in his prose, and together with these an
urbanity, a tenderness, and at times a passion in a vein
entirely his own.   Keats and Landor were both writers of
absolutely unborrowed and original powers, who, if they con-
tributed nothing to its moral and spirtual advancement, are
at least free from any trace of the conventionalisms of the
age.   In Landor's 'Hellenics' we may give ourselves up to
the illusion that we are reading Greek without an effort,
for here indeed

> 'Through the trumpet of a child of Rome
> Rang the pure music of the flutes of Greece.'

In the 'Imaginary Conversations' we mix with society of the
best Italian, Greek, French, Spanish, English, which talks
as eloquently and well, if not better, than it did while it
lived and moved beneath the sun ; and among the occasional
verses, where almost all is unalloyed gold or silver, gleams
at times a gem like this :—

> 'Ah ! what avails the sceptred race !
>   Ah ! what the form divine !
> What every virtue, every grace !
>   Rose Aylmer, all were thine.
>
> Rose Aylmer, whom these wakeful eyes
>   May weep, but never see,
> A night of memories and sighs
>   I consecrate to thee.'

Landor's solitary island, sundered from the mainland, has gathered unto itself treasures brought from far off famous shores; it cannot be left unvisited by any traveller who would know the extent of England's poetic and intellectual wealth.

CHAPTER VI

Moore—Campbell—Wolfe

WITH the entrance of the introspective spirit into modern life has come, among the readers of poetry, an indifference to literature that does not grapple with problems, that is not addressed to the solution of physical and metaphysical questions. The distinctive, moral, and didactic tone of English literature, its prevailing seriousness of aim was lost at one period alone, the period of the Restoration, when the wits and beaux were the men of letters, and the Stuart Court the patron of poetry. The poetry of the Restoration was avowedly a poetry of pleasure. But the spirit of moral purpose reasserted itself almost immediately. The ethical impulse of Pope and Johnson was carried on by Crabbe and Cowper. With the influx of the new tide of thought at the beginning of the present century that impulse was spiritualised and deepened, and in Carlyle we had the high priest of what he himself called 'gospel' literature, literature with a deliberate, moral and spiritual intention. The literature of joy has now been for long out of vogue; a sternness of resolve to deal only with matters of the soul, such as was the motive of the poetry of the Middle Ages like Dante's, has been the mastering force in the nineteenth century. We have been for long in the shadow of a creed almost pessimistic, even when most spiritual, governed by the advice of Goethe,—'Try to understand yourself and things around you.' All this is well : but self-consciousness may occupy too much of life ; and, meanwhile, the wise spirit of cheerfulness has not had due honour done her in the houses of latter-day authors.

There are signs, indeed, of a large and freer ideal, which shall include joy among its duties, for which ideal Browning was a strong champion. It is still, however, doubtful whether, 'As You like It,' or, 'The Midsummer's Night's Dream,' would not, if produced to-day, be deemed frivolous, and beneath the dignity of a great author, and whether Milton's 'L'Allegro,' would be treated as other than a graceful piece of society-verse not at all comparable with a poem wrestling with the psychic evolution of man. Although seriousness of purpose marks the greater portion of the poetry of the early part of this century, the bards of passion condescended at times, as Byron and Moore did, to become bards of mirth, with salutary results for the body politic and social. Besides, by the poetry of mirth, the intellectual and moral stress was relieved by poetry less highly pitched, by verses which appealed to universal instincts, but demanded less activity of imagination, less fulness of emotion on the reader's part, and were thus welcome. What a relief after verse like this, the familiar consuming emotions of Shelley,—

> 'I faint, I perish with my love ! I grow
>   Frail as a cloud whose splendours pale
> Under the evening's ever-changing glow ;
>   I die like mist upon the gale,
>   And like a wave under the calm I fail ; '

or, after this, his familiar politico-religious strain,—

> ' Gray Power was seated
> Safely on her ancestral throne ;
> And Faith, the Python undefeated,
> Even to its blood-stained step dragged on
> Her foul and wounded train, and men
> Were trampled and deceived again,'

to catch the gay lilt of

> ' Who has not heard of the Vale of Cashmere,
> With its roses the brightest that earth ever gave,
> Its temples, and grottos, and fountains as clear
> As the love-lighted eyes that hang over their wave ?

the stir of coming fray in this :—

> ' Pibroch of Donuil Dhu,
> Pibroch of Donuil,
> Wake thy wild voice anew,
> Summon Clan Conuil.'

We expect a poet to be acquainted with, even to be inspired by the highest thought of his own day, but none the less do we expect that the slighter tendencies, the less exalted moods should have their place in the poetry of an epoch. Our theology, and our politics, and our political economy, if we are ready to allow these departments of our intellectual life to be visited by the poet, as well as the department of our emotions, which will include much beside our love affairs—we must suffer him in less arduous hours to tune his lyre to sprightlier measures. Doubtless the minor currents of an epoch will not carry the poet, who trusts to them only, to the main river of lasting song, which flows steadily down the years. That poetry has the best chance of survival, which, in addition to the ideas of the times in which it was produced, contains matter

of permanent human interest ; and poetry has a better
chance of survival than prose, because it presents its matter
in a more permanently interesting, because more intensified,
and impassioned and vital form. The wit and humour
of ' Moore's Rhymes on the Road,' or ' The Fudge Family
in Paris,' have little attraction for the reader of to-day,
they were not in the main stream of the determining
tendencies of the age ; but Moore was not wholly bard
of mirth, and because he was a bard of passion also, he
survives, and will survive.   His reputation was made before
Byron's, he was a popular poet before Shelley's name
was even known ; and because he came before the great
lights of the time, his own has suffered temporary eclipse.
Matthew Arnold has warned us against permitting the
historic estimate of a poet to tinge the real estimate of
him ; but while it may willingly be conceded that Moore
cannot be ranked as his contemporaries ranked him, there
is danger of losing sight of the unquestionable debt owed
to him by his greater successors. Tennyson wrote of his
own contribution to English poetry, and the success of
his imitators,—

> ' Most can raise the flowers now,
>   For all have got the seed.'

And we may say of Moore that his fluid, easy manner, his
introduction and mastery of new metrical forms, his natural
lyrical note, were full of suggestion and teaching to the
poets who followed him. Save what came from Burns,
there had not been heard in England a true song from the
time of the Cavalier and Roundhead campaigns. If he
were not himself a great poet, Moore was undoubtedly the
master from whom many great poets had their first lessons

in the essentials of poetic art, music, and grace of form.   It
it not, perhaps, too much to say that, although infinitely
stronger in every intellectual and poetic quality, Byron owes
the music of his best songs directly to Moore.   It were
hardly misleading to sign the name of Thomas Moore after
these verses, for example :—

> ' O, talk not to me of a name great in story ;
> The days of our youth are the days of our glory ;
> And the myrtle and ivy of sweet two-and-twenty
> Are worth all your laurels, though never so plenty.'

The honeyed smoothness of Moore's melodies does not now
fascinate the ear accustomed to the more complex harmony
of modern artists ; but they were a marvel and a revelation
of the possibilities of language in his own day, and to ears
accustomed to the monotonous tinkle of the heroic couplet
in inferior hands.   Like Scott, Moore did not attempt to
make poetry a vehicle for abstract philosophising, or for the
presentation of theories of the universe.   For this reason,
because he did not choose to make the burden of life's
mystery a brooding presence in his poetry, he is excluded
from the sacred company of the poets, and ranked among
the authors of *vers de société* by the same class of critics who
speak of Macaulay as a writer of clever editorials.   Let it
be granted that sweetness rather than strength is the dis-
tinctive feature of ' Lalla Rookh ' and of the ' Irish
Melodies ;' it was a sweetness recovered to English poetry
after an absence of more than a hundred years, a sweetness
unborrowed and genuine which it could ill have spared.
To appreciate it aright, read over Roger's ' Pleasures of
Memory,' or any other of the poems of this poet, who
carried over into the nineteenth the best traditions of the

eighteenth-century school. 'The winter is past, the rain is over and gone, the flowers appear on the earth ; the time of the singing is come.'

Of the historic and the philosophic tendencies in the poetry of the beginning of the century, Moore, like Southey and Scott, was affected only by the first. The increased interest in man as man, which was involved in the ideas at the root of the movement culminating in the French Revolution, greatly developed the historic sense. The search for the noble or the picturesque in other lands and other ages ministered to the imagination new roused to wider sweeps of wing. Poets went far afield for their subjects ; Byron, Scott and Southey laid European history under contribution, while Moore sought and won the spoils of the East to bejewel his song. Campbell, who was a late follower of the classical and didactic school in his ' Pleasures of Hope,' fell in with the prevailing fashion by writing a romantic narrative poem, ' Gertrude of Wyoming,' whose scene was laid in America. The philosophic or the historic sense mastered all the imaginative minds of the day, and presided over its literature. While the poems which, like Southey's and Byron's tales, or Moore's ' Lalla Rookh,' are revivals of an artificial kind, and inevitably destined to lose their hold upon the public taste within a generation or two of that which welcomed them with a din of applause, those poems which present the thought, the central conceptions which governed men's minds, and which more or less speak the language of the universal man—the man who is not a mere child of his own age—have escaped the withering autumnal breath of time.

Moore is not saved by the ' Loves of the Angels,' or even by ' Lalla Rookh,' brilliant as is the colouring and execu-

tion and fresh as is the narration, he is not saved by the
sparkle of his wit or the piquancy and ingenuity of his per-
sonal satire, but by the ' Irish Melodies ; ' and that because
here alone in his work is he in the main stream of human
interest.   His liberalism, unmixed with the graver philoso-
phic element of a liberalism like Wordsworth's, was, if
narrower in scope, intenser and more enduring in feeling.
The blade of satire he used in the Liberal cause was keen
and searching, but he wielded it like a gentleman who had
learnt his swordsmanship in a chivalric school.   His feelings
are more thoroughly engaged and less under restraint in the
Irish lyrics, than which we have in our language no purer
emotional music.   Though, when Moore sang directly out
of burning love for his own country, his passion is true and
deep, it would be an error to think of him as inspired by the
hot spirit of the Celtic bards.   His lyrics have neither the
fierceness of passion, nor the overpowering dignity of melan-
choly, that marks the genuine bardic songs.   He had the
gay manner of the troubadour, his lightness of heart and
deftness of hand ; but was without the almost terrible inten-
sity of emotion, the pervading unconquerable gloom which
so powerfully impress the reader of ancient Celtic literature.
Burns came much nearer reproducing the weird Gaelic ring
in some of his songs ; he was, at all events, in the direct
line of descent from the ancient minstrels ; whereas Moore
was separated from those of his own land by a gap filled by
no poet—a gap of silence, complete and impassable.   Only
in one sense can the truth of his own words be admitted—

' Dear Harp of my Country ! in darkness I found thee,
   The cold chain of silence had hung o'er thee long,
   When proudly, my own Island Harp, I unbound thee,
   And gave all thy chords to light, freedom and song.'

In the sense that the silence was broken by the voice of a true poet, whose lips were touched by the live coal from off the altar of freedom, the boast is a true one. But the traditions of ancient Irish poetry were not carried on by him ; it was impossible that they should be. The Island poets, to whom Spenser indulgently listened during his Irish exile, and indulgently praised, were an extinct race. To carry on their traditions, the traditions of clan affections or clan hatreds, was no more in his power than to reproduce the conditions of that bygone time. The lively sensibility, the variable temperament, passing in a moment from grave to gay, is Celtic ; and this lively sensibility, this variable temperament, Moore's songs, no less than the record of his life, prove him to have possessed. But the source of the intensity and of the deep underlying melancholy of the true Celtic poetry, the source of its distinctive qualities, was not open to him. The Celtic bards, when they were poets of Nature, were poets of Nature in her wildest and dreariest or most sublime aspects, of Nature in her mountain solitudes, or on her desolate, wave-worn shores, of Nature where the presence of man gave little more than a profound impression of his insignificance. When they were poets of action, it was heroic action such as Homer celebrates, the prowess of chiefs, the vengeance wrought and re-wrought in irreconcilable family feuds ; and if they celebrated a maiden's beauty it was more often to lament the sad fortune that was its dower than the delights of love which were its birthright. In the intensity of a patriotic ode like that beginning,—

> ' When he who adores thee has left but the name
> Of his fault and his sorrows behind ; '

or in the melancholy of that truly beautiful song which

breathes the never-dying sentiment of what is gone never
to return—

> ' Oft, in the stilly night,
>   Ere Slumber's chain has bound me,
> Fond Memory brings the light
>   Of other days around me,—'

in the intensity and the melancholy of these, characteristic as
they are of Moore, there is the emotion of pride without its
hauteur, the tender wistfulness of grief without its grandeur;
but it is the hauteur of their pride and the grandeur of their
sorrow that make the Celtic poets what they are.

Moore is not kept alive by his wit, Campbell is not
remembered for his style; in both patriotic feeling was the
fountain of their enduring songs. Moore and Campbell
were elegant narrators in verse; but mere narration is of no
avail, however crafty or brilliant, with posterity. ' Romances
and novels in verse,' as De Quincey said, 'constitute the
poetry which is *immediately* successful; and that is a poetry,
it may be added, which, being successful through one genera-
tion, afterwards is unsuccessful for ever.'   Immediate and
dazzling success was the lot of ' The Lady of the Lake,'
of ' The Corsair,' of ' Lalla Rookh '; whatever success ' Ger-
trude of Wyoming,' or ' Roderick, the Last of the Goths,'
achieved was immediate; how comes it that such poems as
these pass suddenly from meridian splendour into almost
total eclipse? The question may be put in another way, how
does a novel in verse differ from a poem in the restricted
and in the enduringly successful sense? And it may be an-
swered by saying that the affinity between thought and ex-
pression, the brotherhood of the word and the thing, are not
fully acknowledged by it.   The magical aptness of phrase,
the gift of the only word which makes the poet a sayer of un-

forgettable things, is not always in the power even of the true
poet, if he proceed to put a girdle round the whole world,
or even a vast tract of country. To say the unforgettable
thing, to name, as with divine unfailing instinct, the thing
that men have been vainly endeavouring to name since the
creation of the world,—to do this, or to leave in the reader's
soul, when every word, every detail, has passed from the
memory, a body of inspiring thought, or upon his mental
vision a sculptured image of grouped and unified beauty,
these are not contemplated by, nor are they possible to, the
writer of a novel in verse. 'The Lady of the Lake,' 'Lalla
Rookh,' 'The Corsair,' 'Gertrude of Wyoming,' 'Roderick,
the Last of the Goths,' these are poems dependent for their
interest upon their newness and upon the brilliant colour of
their details. They dealt with lands and peoples romantic
because comparatively or altogether unknown, and the
pleasure they gave was the pleasure of surprise. But
poems which charm by surprise alone, by the unexpected
and the new, are like melodies which catch and fascinate
the ear for an hour or a day, but become intolerable when
they are thoroughly known ; and they are thoroughly known
in a very short time. Great art is easily recognised by its
inexhaustibleness. When we have heard this, for example,
a dozen times, we should greatly prefer not to hear it again—

> ' Not always actions show the man ; we find
> Who does a kindness is not therefore kind.'

When this has rung in our ears for a day, the cadence palls
and tires—

> ' A sensitive plant in a garden grew,
> And the young winds fed it with silver dew,
> And it opened its fan-like leaves to the light,
> And closed them beneath the kisses of night.'

But how of this?—

> ' The wrestling of this world asketh a fall ; '

or this ?—

> ' Come ; we have no friend
> But resolution, and the briefest end.'

There is here the fascination of poetry that is inexhaustible, whose wisdom is never trite, and whose music never palls upon the ear. This is poetry that bears repetition, and not only bears repetition but courts it, and has its charm strengthened by it. Poetry such as 'Lalla Rookh,' or as 'Gertrude of Wyoming,' cannot bear repetition ; repetition takes away from the effect of the freshness and colour which surprised and delighted us at first, and it is upon the effect produced by this freshness and colour that these poems depend for their value and for their interest. Such poems do not say about their subjects all that is essential, and only what is essential ; they say a vast number of things, of fine, picturesque, graceful things : but these are all ineffectually fine, picturesque or graceful, for they are not under the governance of a ruling idea ; they are fortuitous gleams of beauty, not the related beauties which make the perfect face. And it is only the expression of the perfect face, the result of all the related loveliness, not its details, that haunts the memory ; and by his power, we may add, to make his work memorable is the artist known. High poetry is memorable, and it is law-abiding, for, though appearing to move with the most unfettered freedom, the great work of art is also the least lawless, and swings with the untroubled acquiescence of a planet in its governed orbit.

Campbell's lyrics have a sterner ring than Moore's, the

ring of battle.   He is the sounder of England's war-trumpet, whose blare stirs the blood that came to her from the Norse sea-kings, the fighting blood, till it courses and tingles through the veins;—

> ' The meteor flag of England
>   Shall yet terrific burn,
> Till danger's troubled night depart,
>   And the star of peace return.'

His province has never been invaded by another, save in Wolfe's 'Burial of Sir John Moore,' more spontaneous than any of Campbell's lyrics, the only English poem that challenges his supremacy in his own province.   But by far the greater part of Campbell's poetry, like Moore's, was not written directly as a result of the poetic impulse.   Both wrote their longer works, and the same may be said of Southey, after careful historical preparation, with deliberation, uninspired by any divine enthusiasm or the heightened sense of power that accompanies the poetic *afflatus*. Without the inspiring breath, whose coming and going are not within his control, and the presence or absence of which the poet is not always conscious of, art is expended in vain, the vital essence is wanting to the poem, and it fails to communicate that elevated feeling of delight, the quick responsive thrill which corresponds to the higher creative pleasure of the artist himself.   Of all the novels in verse written at this period, with the exception of Scott's, perhaps those in 'Lalla Rookh' may fairly be said to be still the most readable, and to be the most likely to secure more than occasional readers in the future.   Its oriental splendours, the intrinsic interest of its stories, the relief afforded by its dainty humour, the music and perfumes of the East that hang about it, force us to give 'Lalla Rookh' a place apart from the historic tales and foreign romances with which it is usually and not altogether incorrectly classed. While not a work of high genius, it is far beyond the reach of writers of talent. Moore, like his greater countryman, Goldsmith, had the genial art of making lasting friends of his readers; the impulsive tenderness, the intermingled humour and pathos, the entrance of the Irish accent are irresistible. The epicurean element in Moore weakens his poetry while it lends to it a certain attractiveness.

The absence of any attractive graces, despite the purity of style and motive in Campbell, will effectually prevent his longer works from becoming again what they once were—popular favourites. Campbell's career well illustrates the poetic revolution of the century. The ' Pleasures of Hope' is refined pseudo-classic verse, untouched by the warm airs of spring that broke up the frost that bound English poetry, and had nearly wrought a complete silence by congealing its very sources ; ' Gertrude of Wyoming' has the romantic flavour of the foreign novel; but in the ballads, the war lyrics, and in 'O'Connor's Child,' the new spirit flashes out its passionate flames, and lifts Campbell at once from an imitator of Goldsmith to a rank which entitled him to his rest in Westminster Abbey.

Perhaps Moore was the greater poet. These distinctions matter not; they are questions for the literary schoolmen, or for wit-combats on winter evenings. In that corner of a nation's heart, which it keeps closest from view, but cherishes the more jealously, the corner which holds its filial love for the mother-land of its traditions and history, Campbell and Moore have their rightful place. Our Lares and Penates may not be the greatest gods, but they are the gods of our hearths and homes.

CHAPTER VII

POETRY AND ITS JUST LIMITATIONS

Shelley

THE wide-sweeping movement of thought, of which the French Revolution was the most striking product, the movement towards a reconstruction of society with the watchword 'Liberty, Equality, Fraternity,' gives us the key to the motives and substance of the greater portion of English poetry written since the time of Burns. Beginning as an abstract theory, the result of philosophic observations on existing social conditions, it spread to the masses, and became a creed based upon emotional conviction, and ultimately blazed, in France, into revolutionary action. England, a country slower to act, as well as, perhaps, to be convinced, did not afford so rich a soil for a theory in germ ; and the progress of the ideas which had been circulating in European literature for a hundred years, was here very gradual. A few of the more imaginative English minds, like that of Wordsworth, were inflamed with the hope that these ideas would bring in their train the supreme renovation of society, and usher in the golden age for which mankind had so long and so eagerly and so vainly looked. With the collapse of the Revolution in France came to most of these minds, among others to Wordsworth's, disillusion ; he was the great 'lost

leader' of the democratic cause. Some few of the dis-
appointed hopers possessed their souls in peace, and did
not altogether despair that out of evil might come good;
believing that although Utopia could not be built in a day,
the generous impulses awakened, the enthusiasm aroused in
the cause of a nobler social and political life could not
altogether die away or be expended in air, but would in
time, like the little leaven, work out the lofty ideal of a
perfected society. Shelley, perhaps alone of all the higher
minds of the time, was unmoved by the failure of abstract
theory in the sphere of practice; and he was so unmoved
because he was not born until after the Revolution, and
never came face to face with its convincing realities.
For this reason, and because recorded facts never weighed
appreciably in the balance with him against a theory to
which he was emotionally drawn, he stands out conspicuous
not only as an embodiment of the pure revolutionary spirit,
but of that spirit victorious in defeat, a phœnix arising from
its own ashes.

As we look back upon that time, a time of which
Wordsworth cried,—

> 'Joy was it in that dawn to be alive,
> But to be young was very heaven,'

we find it hard to realise the passionate expectation, the
strong and almost childlike trust that filled the minds and
hearts of its more thoughtful and earnest men. We, cer-
tainly, have experienced no such wave of joyful emotion,
lifting us by anticipation into an earthly paradise; rather
we have felt the recoil of defeat, the hopelessness of
indulging in dreams. We, in our most sanguine moments,
are sceptical of the reality of our progress towards higher

and better things ; and the most representative poet of the
latter .half of this century, Tennyson, so far from feeling
that the goal of human progress is at hand, comforts
himself, saves himself from despair, by the thought that the
race is yet in its infancy, that it is the dawn of better things
we see,—

              ' Dawn not day !
Is it shame, so few should have climbed from the dens in the level
    below,
Men, with a heart and a soul, no slaves of a four-footed will ?
But if twenty million of summers are stored in the sunlight still,
We are far from the noon of man, there is time for the race to grow.

              ' Red of the dawn !
Is it turning a fainter red ?   So be it, but when shall we lay
The ghost of the brute that is walking and haunting us yet, and be
    free ?
In a hundred—a thousand winters ?   Oh, what will *our* children be,
The men of a hundred thousand, a million summers away ? '

A different gospel this from that preached by the poets
of the Revolution ! the fire and flame have gone out of
it ; we are not summoned here to the festival that cele-
brates victory, but to a long and weary campaign, the end
of which we can never hope to see.   It is natural for us
—who have not felt the power of the movement of which
we have been speaking, but on the contrary, have realised
the terrible slowness of the advance, the bewildering diffi-
culties, the inevitable delays that must accompany it — it
is natural that we should regard with some impatience the
songs in anticipation of triumph sung by the poets, to the
sentiments of which our minds are not attune, and that
we should treat with a certain contemptuous scorn their
childlike optimistic philosophies political or social.   In the

effort to estimate aright the worth of the poetry of Shelley, it must be remembered, if we are to do justice, that it is the voice of a singularly intense and simple nature that the fervour and the passion which speak in it were very real, and that its creed was felt with entire conviction. Though we may be in a sense sadder and wiser, we must be on our guard against a summary dismissal of Shelley as a philosophic teacher. Why deal at all, some-one may ask, with the philosophic value of his poetry? Why not treat it simply as an art-product? Critics there are who consistently disregard a poet's teaching, critics who are the advocates of 'art for art's sake;' but if we are willing to abide by Plato's decision and make the chief enquiry regarding a poet's work not 'Is it pleasurable?' but 'Is it useful to states and to human life?' an examination of Shelley's poetry as 'art' will not content us. Opinions differ, however, as to the value of Shelley's poetry, not only in relation to life, but even as regards form and the qualities that give pleasure. Opinions, indeed, differ upon the precise rank to be assigned to most poets; opinions are guided by taste, and will differ more or less while the world lasts. But in spite of divergences of taste, and the existence of what we may term 'preferences,' when we come to look closely into the matter we find that most thoughtful and cultivated men are agreed respecting the merits, the striking qualities, the worth for life, of the work of the world's best poets. With Shelley it is not so. There is no poet, perhaps, about whom critical opinions are so divergent, and so widely divergent. The mass of opinion is indisputably in his favour, the majority is with him; but the minority is a strong minority, and famous names appear in it. The more enthusiastic

of the majority, its leaders, regard the poetry of Shelley
as in many ways the most perfect of all poetry that ever
was written, and speak of the poet himself in terms
borrowed from the language of religious worship. The
minority, while admitting the extraordinary character of
his genius, believe that his poetic work is a comparative
failure — a magnificent failure if you will—but compara-
tively with the poetry of the men beside whom he is
ranked by the majority, an undeniable failure. Take Mr
Swinburne's estimate of him as representing the judgment
of the majority: 'Shelley outsang all poets on record but
some two or three throughout all time; his depths and
heights of inner and outer music are as divine as Nature's,
and not sooner exhaustible. He was alone the perfect
singing god; his thoughts, words, deeds, all sang together
. . . the master singer of our modern race and age;
the poet beloved above all other poets, being beyond all
other poets; in one word—and the only proper word—
divine . . . he holds the same rank in lyric as Shake-
spere in dramatic poetry—supreme and without a second of
his race. . . . Of all forms or kinds of poetry the two
highest are the lyric and the dramatic, and as clearly as
the first place in the one rank is held among us by
Shakespere, the first place in the other is held—and will
never be resigned—by Shelley.' After this, one needs a little
time to recover breath; especially does an adherent of the
judgment of the minority, as expressed by Matthew Arnold,
need it: 'The right sphere for Shelley's genius was the
sphere of music, not of poetry; the medium of sounds he can
master, but to master the more difficult medium of words
he has neither intellectual force enough nor sanity enough.'
'In poetry no less than in life he was a beautiful and

ineffectual angel, beating in the void his luminous wings in vain.' Here is indeed divergence, and that with a vengeance !—not between critics merely, but between critics who are also excellent poets. We are assured by Mr Swinburne, in his most oracular vein, that upon the twin-peaked Parnassus sit Shakespere and Shelley, the gods of dramatic and of lyric poetry; and upon enquiry at another oracle, we are asked to believe that Shelley's proper sphere was not at all the sphere of poetry, but of music, that he is 'a beautiful but ineffectual angel, beating in the void his luminous wings in vain.' Further argument is not needed to convince us of the irreconcilable nature of the quarrel between the majority and the minority respecting Shelley's place among the poets. All men, and therefore all lovers of poetry, dislike to be out of sympathy with their friends, out of touch on any point with those who are of their chosen companionship, and it happens, therefore, that many fall in with the popular verdict—the verdict of the majority upon Shelley—without any sincere personal conviction ; without having experienced such a rapture, for instance, as is expressed by Mr Swinburne in connection with this line of Shelley's—

* ' Fresh spring, and summer, and winter hoar.'

' The music of this line, taken with its context—the melodious effect of its exquisite inequality—I should have thought was a thing to thrill the veins and draw tears to

* The context is—

> ' Out of the day and night
> A joy has taken flight ;
>   Fresh spring, and summer, and winter hoar
> Move my faint heart with grief, but with delight
>   No more—Oh, never more !'

the eyes of all men whose ears were not closed against all harmony by some denser and less removable obstruction than shut out the song of the Sirens from the hearing of the crew of Ulysses.' To experience these ecstasies, this more than lively gratification, from the poetry of Shelley is probably not the lot of all those who constitute the majority in his favour, and it may therefore be in reality merely a nominal majority. But however these things are, it seems very evident that all verdicts on Shelley are likely to be personal, the record of personal satisfaction or personal disappointment, and thus not disinterested. And perhaps the best way of ensuring the justice of the final verdict of the incorruptible court of posterity is for each person who undertakes to speak about Shelley to speak freely and frankly, without affectation, and without fear, giving his own personal impressions, as pure as may be from admixture of foreign prejudice. In order that what is here said on Shelley may be seen clearly to attempt no more than such a personal estimate, it will be best to speak in the first person, and to begin by the avowal that the present writer does not belong to the majority spoken of above, believing that no one can belong to it 'who would have,' as Plato says, 'poetry appear at her best and truest.' I shall endeavour in what I have to say to convey the impressions a perusal of Shelley's poetry gives me, and I may perhaps anticipate my general conclusion by putting its main result in this way. I believe that anyone who finds the highest poetry in Shakespere can never grow to look upon Shelley as, in any respect, a poet of the first rank ; or, to speak more accurately, that as Shakespere becomes more and more to a reader of poetry, Shelley becomes less and less. I am here speaking of Shakespere not as an isolated peak of solitary splendour, but as typical of those poets who are, in one word, *mundane*, who take to do with the world as it is, and abide cheerfully by its limitations. 'The greatest artists of the world,' as Bagehot truly said, 'have ever shown an enthusiasm for reality. To care for notions and abstractions, to philosophise, to reason out conclusions, to care for schemes of thought, are signs in the artistic mind of secondary excellence. A Schiller, a Euripides, a Ben Jonson, cares for *ideas* —for the parings of the intellect and the distillation of the mind ; a Shakespere, a Homer, a Goethe, finds his mental occupation, the true home of his natural thoughts, in the real world—"which is the world of all of us"—where the face of Nature, the moving masses of men and women, are ever changing, ever multiplying, ever mixing one with the other.' Shelley, for this reason, I never read without disappointment. So far from any enthusiasm for reality, he betrays an absolute repugnance to it ; he cares only for ideas, for abstractions, for philosophising, and—it may hardly be breathed above a whisper—he philosophises badly, though brilliantly. What was his philosophy, and how has he contributed to its efficacy ? Shelley's youth was an unhappy one, for among his schoolfellows the strange, sensitive boy was misunderstood and subjected to a cruel and persistent persecution. Of a dreamy temperament and gentle disposition, he had nothing in common with the average English schoolboy, and in his earliest thoughts were mingled indignation at injustice and hatred of tyranny. At Eton and Oxford he was deep in science and in the Greek poets ; but his studies were pursued without method, and the real bent of his mind displayed itself in the hold which Godwin's book on 'Political Justice' took upon it, and in his attraction to metaphysical philosophy.

Lucretius was his first master, Hume came later as his philosophical guide, and Plato, whom he never came near understanding as philosopher, but followed with keen delight in his flights of poetic mysticism, Plato was the source of the 'notions' of his later poetry.

It is a long journey from the materialism of Lucretius to the idealism of Plato, but it was a trifle to the winged feet of the poet. Indeed, Shelley was never either materialist or idealist, and he came nearer being both at one and the same time than perhaps has ever before been permitted to mortal. He hurried from system to system, as a bee flies from flower to flower, taking from each such ideas as were congenial to his own mind. It was a mind not formed to move within the confines of any system; systematic investigation was altogether alien to it. Powerfully original as that mind was, it belonged to the common class, which, when emotionally attracted by an idea or a proposition, instantly hands in its adherence to it. For the patient sifting, the quiet persistent investigation, which precedes intellectual assent in the true thinker, he had no faculty. The processes of his mind were like lightning in rapidity, his intuitions were peculiarly true, his thought added little of value to them. In so far as belief involves intellectual assent, quite apart from emotional, Shelley can hardly be said to have had any beliefs. Precision in thinking exercised no tyranny over him, as it does over the minds of scientific investigators; it was unnecessary to him, as it seems to be unnecessary to the great majority of men. But he was the impassioned prophet of the purer ideal of the Revolution which had survived the wreck of its less noble accompaniments; a generous, high-hearted hope for man beats, despite all his aberrations of judgment, in every line

K

of his poetry.   If he were not a sure thinker, and a sure
thinker he was not, a sincerer spiritual fervour never ani-
mated the herald of any cause.   But to say so is to increase
the disappointment with which we answer the question,
How far has he contributed to the efficacy of the cause he
had at heart, and for which he aspired to be the harbinger
of its later and truer spring?   What remains with us in the
end?   The momentary thrill passes, and difficulty and
incredulity are again our companions; there has been
given us no sustaining spiritual food.   To me Shelley's
advent and career, rapid, dazzling, so soon quenched, re-
semble the advent and career of one of those wayward
lights of heaven that takes for a time our eyes from the
moon and stars, and holds them fixed upon itself, as it out-
shines all other splendours.   He was the comet that blazed
forth the death of empires and the birth of the accepted day
of freedom.   To be the personified ardour of a great cause,
such as in person and in work Shelley was, is one thing; to
be a lasting succour to the hearts of men in every mood,
in every accident, is another, a widely different thing.   'It
is of little moment,' as Emerson tells us, 'that one or two
or twenty errors in our social system be amended, but of
much that the man be in his senses.'   How admirably true,
and penetrating to the root of all social disorders.

   But Shelley's conclusions, the conclusions which deter-
mined his actions and appear as the ruling principles of his
poetic thought, were not the conclusions of sanity; they were
such as recommended themselves to his emotions, and his
emotions were very inflammable and very strong.   Without
possessing at any period of life definite beliefs, he had no
basis of thought or action; he had no starting-point, no
port of departure on the voyage for the discovery of truth,

and his intellectual position was out of all reckoning. A man may emancipate himself from the beliefs he has held as a child or at any subsequent period of youth; but unless he have a centre from which to pursue his enquiries, his own opinions will for long remain a puzzle perhaps even to himself. Shelley's whole life was a series of impulses, and impulses are fatal to reason.* The wise man recognises that the crowd of desires, external incentives to action, and internal impulses, must be brought before the central court of the controlling governing self for adjudication. He does not dream of satisfying a desire, or pursuing any chance object of the outward world without previous enquiry into the intrinsic worth of the object, or the wisdom and justice of satisfying the desire. But Shelley never realised the duality of man's nature; an impulse was to be followed because it existed; an opinion, because he felt strongly its truth, was to be instantly translated into action. The recognition of the central seat of government in man does not come in childhood, it is gradually acquired, as we find that choices between various courses of action are offered to us, and as we come to exercise the highest faculty of man as a free agent. But into this noble inheritance of perfected manhood can we say that Shelley ever entered? Remaining a child, free range was given to his nature; unrestrained and uncontrolled he followed whithersoever the fancy of the moment led him. In such licence there is unlimited scope for wickedness as well as for high and generous action. Shelley was by nature gentle and magnanimous, largehearted, and free-handed; but these are not virtues, they are simply gifts of Nature; and it is only to deliberately

* For a masterly examination of Shelley's nature, see Bagehot's *Literary Studies*, vol. i.

willed actions that we attach praise or blame, for with the
will we enter the sphere of morals. We may best conceive
of Shelley's life as lived in a sphere apart from morals; in
temperament he was, perhaps, as his admirers would say,
divine ; but temperament is a small matter in the world of
men compared with character. Character pertains to man
as the denizen of an ethical world : but of an ethical world
Shelley does not seem to have been conscious, of an ethical
world there is no note in his poetry. When it is said that
he lived in a sphere apart from morals, in a non-ethical
sphere, it is not said that it was an immoral sphere. Certain
spiritual principles regulate it; what, exactly, it were hard to
say; they are never defined for the mind, but are the sub-
jects of the passionate devotion of the soul. They are not,
at all events, principles suited to guide the erring steps of
the human race, which has enough to confuse it already in
its dim gropings after truth and reality. And, indeed,
Shelley himself seems to have been scarcely human, and we
are tempted to give this easy explanation of the complex
knot of his nature. He lived, for the most part, in so far as
he was original and striking, in a sphere remote from the
world of men, the actual world, and yet he was no inhabi-
tant of the purely intellectual world of the scientific or
scholarly recluse. In a world of his own creation, supported
and surrounded by the web, which, like the spider's, was
spun out of his own being, and with but frail and slight
connexions to the framework of the real and eternal world,
he lived an original poet, in every sense of the word. There
is a form of originality, however, which is well-nigh profit-
less. To pass by with contempt the capitalised experience
of humanity is to start the race of life some thousands of
years behind your competitors ; a fact which it is difficult to

evade, even when we are assured, as Shelley assures us in his preface to the 'Revolt of Islam,' that—'Love is celebrated everywhere as the sole law which should govern the moral world.' When we read a poem like 'Rosalind and Helen,' we are again reminded of a sentence of Plato's—'You have often seen what a poor appearance the tales of poets make when stripped of the colours which music puts upon them, and recited in prose. They are like faces which were never really beautiful, but only blooming, and now the bloom of youth has passed away from them.' Shelley was as contemptuous of received tradition and authority in matters of social *régime*, as of the practice of the great artists in keeping the solid ground of the real and actual beneath their feet. When one comes to differ from the opinions which have grown and strengthened with the progress of civilisation, which have been sifted and accredited by the best minds, when one abandons the world of experience for the creation of newer and better, good reasons are demanded, reasons which may be broadly described as other than poetic. Not out of clouds and sunbeams can a renovated society be constructed, but out of the very materials of which the present society is composed. Shelley's passion for reform was ardent and sincere; but without formative power, without a knowledge of society and its history, passion for reform leads nowhither. History was Shelley's aversion, it savoured too much of the fact. The fact, indeed, is a more than ordinarily conspicuous element in history, and distaste for it is significant of a distaste for realities. Realities are unpleasantly difficult matters to deal with; their edges and outlines appear so sharply through any covering veil, that they do not lend themselves to be woven into beautiful textures as do the dreams of the imagination ; they offer a stubborn resistance to poetic treatment. But for this reason are the great poets great, that they deal with reality as if it were the most malleable of materials; reality is as potter's clay in their hands, to mould and fashion into pure and lovely, or noble and majestic forms.

But someone may very naturally ask,—'Is it not permissible for the poet to lift the soul of man from out the din and dust of the actual world into a serener air, to speak to him of ideals on which mortal eyes have never rested, to give a wing to his better aspirations that they may soar beyond the familiar and uninspiring presentations to eye and ear of common life?' It is a pertinent question. If the office of the poet be in truth a sacred one, he is something more than a recorder of facts; he is a revealer of the spiritual world. But where lies the spiritual world, the land to which the soul would go? Is it not a world that interpenetrates the real? is, if I may so say, more real than the real? It is not to be thought of as hung aloft between the sun and moon. Shelley's poetry does not, I think, conduct us to the spiritual world ; it leads us away from the real world in which our lot is cast, and, in so doing, leads us away from the spiritual world also, which is only the present world looked at from another side. In his poetry, to use his own words,—

> ' We sail on, away, afar,
> Without a course, without a star,
> But by the instinct of sweet music driven.'

We are borne (who knows how?) to a land of dreams remote from all that is familiar to us. We pass through it and marvel at its strange beauties, its wondrous colours, and undreamt-of shapes; but in it there is nothing which on our return haunts our memories for ever, bringing strength in weakness, courage in adversity, consolation in suffering, wisdom in perplexity. And it is a sad world withal. There is about it an atmosphere of disquiet, of aching desire, of unsatisfied longing. How could it well be otherwise, seeing that Shelley himself, not really conscious of what he desired in art or life, was ever hungering and thirsting after the unattainable, after he knew not what; and was forced to content himself with exquisite thrills of emotion, was forced to make a series of feelings, as the Germans say, his Endzweck? The palpitating and feverish emotions of Shelley have nothing in common with the calm pleasures and majestic pains of minds in serene possession of themselves like those of Sophocles, of Dante, and of Shakespere. These are the true helpers of humanity. I do not say that Shelley gives us nothing, but in comparison with these strong guides, he is a blind leader of the blind. Life was indeed teaching him many things, and would have taught him more; but the lessons were cut short by that sudden squall on the Bay of Spezzia, and the poetry that would have ranked with the great poetry of the world was never written. In the last stanzas of ' Hellas,' composed the year before his death, we have a note rarely before heard in his poetry, simple and direct, a promise of what would have come in after years.

> ' A brighter Hellas rears its mountains
> From waves serener far,
> A new Peneus rolls his fountains
> Against the morning star,
> Where fairer Tempes bloom, there sleep
> Young Cyclads on a sunnier deep.

A loftier Argo cleaves the main,
Fraught with a later prize ;
Another Orpheus sings again,
And loves and weeps and dies.
A new Ulysses leaves once more
Calypso for his native shore.'

This is not the gossamery web of Shelley's most dis-
tinctive style.   I know that this is not his ' divine ' style ; the
style which endears him to his worshippers.   There is here
something akin to the direct purity and simplicity of great
art ; but what Shelley's devotees prefer, what ' thrills their
veins and brings tears to their eyes,' is a strain like this
from ' Epipsychidion ' :—

' Alas, I then was nor alive nor dead ;—
For at her silver voice came Death and Life,
Unmindful each of their accustomed strife,
Masked like twin babes, a sister and a brother.
The wandering hopes of one abandoned mother,
And through the cavern without wings they flew,
And cried—'' Away, he is not of our crew ? ''
I wept, and though it be a dream, I weep.

What storms then shook the ocean of my sleep,
Blotting that Moon, whose pale and waning lips
Then shrank as in the sickness of eclipse ;—
And how my Soul was as a lampless sea,
And who was then its Tempest ; and when She,
The Planet of that hour, was quenched, what frost
Crept o'er those waters, till from coast to coast
The moving billows of my being fell
Into a death of ice, immovable ;—
And then—what earthquakes made it gape and split,
The white moon smiling all the while on it,
These words conceal :—if not, each word would be
The key of staunchless tears.   Weep not for me !'

When Shelley writes in this self-apocalyptic style, he is regarded by the majority as 'the master singer of our modern race and age, the perfect singing god, the poet beloved above all other poets, being beyond all other poets; in one word, and the only proper word, divine.'   But we who cannot discern how this is 'useful to states and to human life' are not thrilled by it, and do not weep.   We are disappointed that a poet with the power which Shelley undoubtedly possessed, did not more worthily employ it; and we are inclined to say that, like Wordsworth, because, like Wordsworth, he was without humour, he never attained to 'the profound conception that there is such a thing as nonsense.'   In so far as Shelley was the prophet of a new faith, the gospel of the universal brotherhood of man, of the set of the tide towards the universal reign of love, and in so far as he was successful in impressing the beauty and nobility of that idea, he was and is an undeniable force.   But in so far as he failed to show how the idea might be realised, in so far as he merely surrounded the central idea with an arabesque of ingenious patterns, a coruscation of lovely colours, in so far as his poetry is only a revelation of the peculiarly fanciful moods of his own mind, he sinks to inferior rank.   In the central motive of his poetry there is force; but that motive was not his own.   The idea was one which had been slowly evolving in the world's thought for centuries: the question is, How far was it advanced by the advocacy of the poet?   In how much did he render it a service by the halo he threw around it?   The service was one of glorification only.   Upon the chaos of social problems his mind emitted strange gleams of visionary light, some are bold to think as misleading as the marsh-fires of a night of storm, but no enduring and steady guiding ray.   His was not the power which out of Chaos makes Kosmos. The philosophy of Shelley's poetry, then, I would say, has the fatal defect of leaving us where we were. The banner of the faith is not advanced by the hymns sung in its honour. We are no further on our way to the ideal commonwealth they celebrate, nor do we even conceive it in firmer, less wavering, outline than of old.

If this were all, it might nevertheless be conceded that as lyrist, as poetic artist, Shelley ranked as it is insisted by the majority that he does rank. Grant that his philosophy is visionary, someone may suggest, What of his lyric gift? What of his pure flame of song, his intense and penetrating cry, the true music of the rejoicing and suffering heart? Must not his lyrics, expressive of emotion, the deep and strong impulses common to human nature, arrest and hold the attention and admiration of all lovers of poetry? And, perhaps, the answer here will be affirmative, but affirmative with limitations. For, just as in the case of his philosophy, the personal estimate is apparently the only possible estimate; and I, for my part, am willing to think with Matthew Arnold that Shelley's 'true sphere was music, that the medium of sounds he could master, but to master the more difficult medium of words he had neither intellectual force enough nor sanity enough.' To put it in another way, Shelley's ideas, his imagery, his words, are all arbitrary, not inevitable. His images come upon us and surprise us, but our delight ceases with the surprise they create; they do not sink into our minds or enrich them by adding to the truths there held sacred. Not infrequently, as in 'Epipsychidion,' does Shelley indulge in the language of uninterrupted metaphor, and not infrequently his similes have no real likeness to their original, but by an ingenious freak of fancy are made to resemble it.

Take for example the concluding similes of the famous four in the 'Skylark.' Exquisite as these pictures are in themselves, they have no vitality as similes; they do not flash their truthfulness upon the mind, they are not inevitable but arbitrary; and we know that, with the exercise of a little further ingenuity, many others equally good might have been added. 'Diction,' says Aristotle, 'composed of metaphors, becomes an enigma; for the essence of an enigma consists in putting together things apparently inconsistent and impossible, and at the same time saying nothing but what is true.' Thus it is that Shelley's poetry is often enigmatical. It is wanting in the lucidity of the best diction, it trangresses into the sphere of music, which is the sphere of unbroken symbol. Neither simile nor metaphor serves its due end unless it elucidates in some way the original which it illustrates. Shelley's words, too, are not inevitable; they are not marshalled, as by an enchanter's wand, to the only places possible for them, which could not be occupied by others. This is a hard saying, and I would not give it utterance if to me it did not seem indisputable. His effects are almost invariably musical effects, unaccompanied by effects of another order, of the intellectual order. Compare with the 'Ode to the Skylark' Keats' 'Ode to the Nightingale.' When I do so, and ask myself which of these two poems comes nearer the inevitable tone of good poetry, which is the more spontaneous song, there is but one answer possible. The impression made by Keats' poem is the impression made by a passage from Shakespere; it leave sthe feeling that it is a flower which has grown up naturally out of the soil of the human mind when the due season came for its appearance. The impression left by the 'Ode to the Skylark' is that of a beautiful and ingenious mosaic of tinted fancies, the pattern of which might have been varied at the pleasure of the artist, without either adding to or taking from the poem as a whole. Not that that poem was constructed as a mosaic is, it came straight from the poet's heart with the swiftness and glow of genuine inspiration; but the god of song did not grant to Shelley the 'natural magic' of Keats, or that astonishing sureness of style—that perfect accuracy of diction which was Milton's birthright.

What shall be said of his imagination? for by his imagination is a poet known. The chief of living as well as of Shelley critics, Professor Dowden, has said that, in imaginative splendour, the 'Faust' of Goethe is inferior to the 'Prometheus Unbound.' It may be so; but to me it seems that Shelley, like his own 'Skylark,' soars and sings, but does not, as Milton does, on the eagle's pinion bear his reader with him. The 'Prometheus' is not comparable as an effort of imagination with the 'Faust'; the actions are on different planes, it is more fitly compared with the 'Paradise Lost.' In the company, and under the guidance of Milton, I see for myself all that the poet saw; with Shelley, I am told of what he sees, but his visions fail to form themselves before my eyes; his characters do not group themselves as those of Shakespere do, they are as impalpable as the mists of dawn. 'Of course,' as Bagehot said, 'all his works contain "Spirits," "Phantasms," "Dream No. 1," and "Fairy No. 3"; but these do not belong to this world.' We may go further and say that they do not belong to any world; certainly not to the

world of vitalising art, for not even in the world of art can
life be given by pronouncing a name. Ariel and Puck,
Titania and Oberon, or the gods of the Attic drama or of
Homer, have no human blood in their veins, but they are
none the less alive, beings created and existent. Withdraw
the 'spirits' from Shelley's world (excluding the 'Cenci'),
and you depopulate it altogether; its inhabitants, like all
its interests, are unreal or fictitious.

We are sometimes told that Shelley evolved a new·
Pantheon, that he created and peopled a new world
comparable to that created in the Greek mythology. To
say so is to betray an incapacity for historic as well as
for literary judgment. Myths are the outcome of the
imagination of the childhood of races, they are a rudi-
mentary form of thought suitable to peoples who have
not advanced beyond simple outlines in their intellectual
drawing. They are valuable because they represent *real*
beliefs—the beliefs of a race in their simplest and most
direct form. The Greek myths are deeply interesting to us
because they embody the thought of the Hellenic people
in their earliest stage of development, their thought upon
every subject in which the human mind finds pleasure or
interest; and embody it as the peculiar genius of that people
alone could have done. The mythology which Shelley left
us has, of course, no such historic value. Myths invented
by a fanciful poet have no weight or dignity beside those
which are the outcome of a whole people's accumulated
mental experience; and when that people is the Hellenic
people, the comparison becomes merely grotesque.

It is, however, as a poet of passion, of pure lyric feel-
ing, to quote the majority once more, that Shelley is unsur-
passed; and we are referred to a passage such as this :—

' I pant for the music that is divine,
My heart in its thirst is a dying flower,
Pour forth the sound like enchanted wine,

Loosen the notes in a silver shower ;
Like a herbless plain for the gentle rain
I gasp, I faint, till they wake again.'

Or this, from the close of ' Epipsychidion,'—

' Woe is me !
The winged words on which my soul would pierce
Into the height of Love's own universe,
Are chains of lead around its flight of fire—
I pant, I sink, I tremble, I expire ! '

Or the close of the beautiful ' Lines to an Indian Air,'

' O lift me from the grass,
I die, I faint, I fail.'

This with Sappho would be pardonable, natural perhaps, in the work of a woman poet, and this is for the majority the ideal expression of the highest lyric passion.   But we who are still for the poetry that is, ' useful to states and to human life,' who would have ' poetry appear at her best and truest,' who are anxious to set apart for the highest honours the poets who give us ' the rhythms of a courageous and harmonious life,' we cannot but think that Plato would have regarded all this as unhealthy in the highest degree. We cannot, indeed, ourselves connect this constant gasping, fainting, failing and expiring, with a great and noble personality.   Intensity of lyrical feeling could not, we think, have hurried Milton or Dante or Sophocles into this strain, into indulging this vulgar abandonment of emotion.   As Mr Aubrey de Vere finely writes :—

' Grief should be
Like joy, majestic, equable, sedate.'

We of the minority feel assured that of such a poet, or of a poet so long as he continued to write in this strain, Plato would have said as he did of the other poets who were excluded from the ideal commonwealth, — 'When one of these makes a proposal to exhibit himself and his poetry, we will fall down and worship him as a sweet and holy and wonderful being; but we must also inform him that there is no place for such as he is in our state— the law will not allow them.   And so when we have anointed him with myrrh, and set a garland of wool upon his head, we shall send him away to another city.   For we mean to employ for our soul's health the rougher and severer poet or story-teller, who will imitate the style of the virtuous only.'

Carlyle said of De Quincey that it was a miserable thing for a man to make a literary reputation out of his vices. There is something about the lyric poetry of Shelley that suggests a somewhat similar idea.   Putting it simply, I think he may be said to have made the most of his sorrows.   'His cry,' said Carlyle, 'is like the infinite, inarticulate wailing of forsaken infants.'   It is all abandonment; we never seem to catch a note that nerves the soul, rather we are unnerved; and how can we remain faithful to poetry that has no nerving power?   'Only that is poetry which cleanses and mans me.'*   In the utterances of Shelley's most inspired words there is frequently, as a critic says of Mr Swinburne, 'nothing to hold or to keep in all the meteor-like shower of words upon words, thoughts upon thoughts, similes upon similes.'   There is, indeed, in Shelley little to have or to hold, and poetry in which there is little memorable is poetry in which there is little

* Emerson.

available for life. The supreme thing in poetry is to preserve intellectual precision amid emotional excitement. Passion is usually inarticulate. But the greatness of the best tragic art of Greece, of the art of Dante, of the art of Shakespere, its conspicuous nobility, is that these artists, as Hamlet says to the players, 'in the very torrent, tempest and, as I may say, whirlwind of their passion acquire and beget a temperance that give it smoothness.' But Shelley's eloquence, his flame of emotion, like his passion for reform, burns hot, without moderation, and leads nowhither. How the keen steel of a sentence like this cuts sheer through the mass of shallow worship of Shelley as a philosophic poet, 'The reader is fatigued with admiration, but is not yet master of his subject.'*

I cannot but feel that into what I have said on Shelley has entered the spirit of controversy, a spirit which is not, or should not be welcome among the members of a great brotherhood like that of the lovers of literature. What object is gained by speaking in dispraise of Shelley, in confessing dissatisfaction with him, and in so doing laying myself open to the easy reply —

> ' Minds that have nothing to confer
> Find little to perceive ' ?

I have not spoken of Shelley's great and enduring qualities as a poet, because pre-eminently in his case these have been, and are so well and ardently dwelt upon by his admirers that an exposition of them gave place, rightly, I think, to a protest against meaningless idolatry — to a plea for sanity in literary judgments. By speaking of

* Emerson, of Milton's prose works.

Shelley as the fellow of Shakespere we go near losing all standard of criticism altogether; we do wrong, not only to the poets with whom he is mentioned in the same breath, but we do wrong to Shelley also.   Sanity before all things in criticism, no less than sanity before all things in life.   We of the minority do not desire that criticism should be a matter of praising or blaming, but we say we do not find in Shelley what above all else we seek in art —spiritual succour, or spiritual peace.

But when that has been said, what remains?   What, indeed, but to be reconverted to Shelley? to be reconverted to him in order that we may take in him a more temperate and a wiser joy.   And as Professor Dowden truly said, when speaking lately in conversation about him, to be reconverted to Shelley, one only needs to read the 'Ode to the West Wind.'   When its swift splendour meets our eyes, we forget the unreality of Shelley's world, his metaphysics, and all his 'gossamery affectation.'   We are borne by verse like this to the verge of recantation of all our words :—

> ' Make me thy lyre even as the forest is ;
> What if my leaves are falling like its own !
> The tumult of thy mighty harmonies
> Will take from both a deep autumnal tone,
> Sweet though in sadness.   Be thou, spirit fierce,
> My spirit !   Be thou me, impetuous one !
> Drive my dead thoughts over the universe
> Like withered leaves to quicken a new birth !
> And by the incantation of this verse,
> Scatter, as from an unextinguished hearth,
> Ashes and sparks, my words among mankind !
> Be through my lips to unawakened earth
> The trumpet of a prophecy !   O, wind,
> If winter comes, can spring be far behind ? '

This, too, may be said, that some minds there are of a type not common, indeed, but not rare, to whom Shelley will always be more stimulating than poets of less ethereal genius. We bid them hail, for they are pilgrims, though their way is not our way, on the same journey that we ourselves would make to the country of a truer freedom and a fuller light.

I cannot more fittingly close what I have space to say than by a quotation from Mr F. W. H. Myers, who pleads eloquently for Shelley while he admits that all is not well with him. If I have made a petty attempt to practise the trade of the poisoner, here is the antidote.

In answer to the case, as he himself well states it, against Shelley, Mr Myers pleads wisely Shelley's youth and immaturity, and concludes thus :—

'The common religion of all the world advances by many kinds of prophecy, and is spread abroad by the flying flames of pure emotion as well as by the solid incandescence of eternal truth. Some few souls indeed there are —a Plato, a Dante, a Wordsworth—whom we may without extravagance call stars of the spiritual firmament, so sure and lasting seems their testimony to those realities which life hides from us as sunlight hides the depth of heaven. But we affirm that in Shelley, too, there is a testimony of like kind, though it has less of substance and definition, and seems to float diffused in an ethereal loveliness. We may rather liken him to the dew-drop of his own song, which

> " Becomes a winged mist,
> And wanders up the vault of the blue day,
> Outlives the moon, and in the sun's last ray
> Hangs o'er the sea, a fleece of fire and amethyst."

For the hues of sunset also have for us their revelation.
We look, and the conviction steals over us that such a
spectacle can be no accident in the scheme of things;
that the whole universe is tending to beauty, and that
the apocalypse of that crimsoned heaven may not be the
less authentic because it is so fugitive—not the less real
because it comes to us in a phantasy wrought out of light
and air.'

With such a sane and eloquent advocate we cannot but
sympathise more than a little.

CHAPTER VIII

AN EPIC REVIVAL

Southey — Scott — Hogg

To seek inspiration in a past age, to essay a revival of life
that is gone, is admittedly an almost hopeless poetic task.
The mental environment of the present accompanies every
man as closely as his shadow in the sun. It seems, too, as
if the poetic forms of each age are vitally suitable only to
the points of view that were exclusively its own, that to
attempt a resuscitation of distinctive poetic forms is to court
as certain failure as to attempt a revival of the body of
thought to which they served as appropriate garment. The
form of the Elizabethan drama is as unsustainable by a
poet to-day as is that of Attic tragedy. The epic manner
of Homer died with his heroic age, the ballad or the chaunt
of the Trouvère, the refrains of early English songs are no
longer producible though they may be imitated. But a
careful survey of the world's literature makes this manifest,
that while no period of history can ever have its exact
counterpart, epochs which display similar habits of mind,
whose environment approximates in some or in many
respects to that of former epochs, produce a like litera-
ture, a literature approximating in tone and in external
feature to that of the former epochs which they resemble.

164

A scrupulous regard to form, for example, is an unfailing sign of a weakness in substance—of a Neo-Alexandrian epoch, like that of Pope, or of the successors of Tennyson. A seeking abroad for an inspiration which the present time and place fail to afford is equally significant of an era of decadence. He who runs may read such marks as these which connect every wave of literature with some predecessor, which betray the same impulse as it rises and gathers strength and volume, or as it breaks and is finally lost in feathery froth and spray.

To speak of an epic revival is to speak of what is only possible with serious limitations, and even then only possible under conditions approximating to those under which the great epics of the world were composed. Epic poetry is the product of primitive civilisations, unable or unaccustomed to express their thoughts in writing. The traditions of a race preserved in song and ballad, and handed down from father to son, are the material upon which the epic poet works. Usually the greatest national event, the subject of numberless short poems, is appropriated and shaped into a consecutive narrative, which thus becomes the record, the only possible record when writing is unknown, of a nation's early history. Of this kind of national epic, the 'Iliad' and the 'Odyssey' of Homer, and the 'Niebelungenlied' are examples. Such poetry, true national epic poetry, giving a picture of primitive society as it appeared to the generation, which, just about to cross the threshold of what we call civilisation, looked back upon the early history of the race—this true national epic poetry is not to be confused with the poetry written in the epic manner by poets in an age of learning and culture, who, by an effort of imagination, transfer themselves to times long past, or build up a structure wholly imaginary.   Such poetry is only successful when it is written by an imaginative artist of the very first order.   The literature of the world affords two instances of supremely successful accomplishments in the epic manner.   The stately barks launched by Virgil and by Milton still float upon the great waters of Time ; but the shipwrecked epics, who can number? From poems like the ' Iliad,' the ' Odyssey,' and the ' Niebelungenlied ' may be gleaned much important knowledge of the customs and history of the peoples among whom they were composed ; but from poems like the ' Æneid ' or ' Paradise Lost ' no such knowledge is obtainable.   These are not national epics in the same sense as the others, but, however magnificent in conception and treatment, artificial copies of a more natural poetry in which the genius and character of a whole race is mirrored.   Looking back upon an heroic age just passing away, the author or authors of the ' Iliad,' out of the material plentifully supplied in the unwritten traditions, songs and ballads which survived, made a complete and rounded whole.   In that poem the art of a dawning culture is at work upon the life of a society and a state of things which that culture has once and for ever overthrown.   It marks an era of transition, of transition from primitive to civilised conditions.   In it is preserved, and herein lies its incommunicable charm, the innocence of childhood with the adolescence of high artistic power.   It tells us much of the politics, of the family life, of the methods of warfare, of the social customs and of the religious beliefs of an early age.   With such a work there is no analogy in ' Paradise Lost ' or even in the ' Æneid,' each the work of a scholar in an age of culture.

Is there any possible analogy to be found among the long

narrative poems due to the awakened historic sense which
the early years of the present century produced in such
numbers? In 1805 appeared two long narrative poems,
'Madoc' and 'The Lay of the Last Minstrel,' epical in scope,
manner and intention; the former, Southey's work, is an
epic of the study, can we say of the latter that it is at all
comparable with the authentic heroic poem historically
valuable because it is a record of an age known to the
author not mediately through writing, but immediately
through personal contact with it?* The answer cannot be
an altogether decisive one; but we may fairly say that if
anywhere in the history of our own country conditions were
favourable for the production of a poem in any sense
parallel to the national epics of other lands, the conditions
were found in Scotland at the close of the eighteenth cen-
tury, and the parallel exists in the case of the poetry of
Walter Scott. The writing of an authentic epic is quite
as much a matter of conditions and times as of genius.
Southey had unquestionably greater difficulty in massing
and unifying his material for a poem than had Scott. He
gathered his action and details from reading that was far and
wide, the imagination did not greatly serve him, it was not
set to work until the intellect had collected and chosen the
needful bricks or quarried stone out of which the edifice
was to be builded. Scott's material lay around him; from the
first his imagination was in play. He had no need to wait
for facts, they were supplied in the very atmosphere he
breathed from childhood; for from childhood ballad poetry,
the tales of the Border, the life of the northern clans, were
the breath of his intellectual life. Before he could read he

* For an interesting article on this subject see Principal Shairp's
'Homeric Spirit in Walter Scott.'—*Aspects of Poetry*, p. 377.

had been taught the ballad of 'Hardicanute.' His early and most impressionable years were passed in a district of which it has been said, 'Every field has its battle and every rivulet his song.' And so in a very special sense he stands, as Homer stood, on the verge of an heroic age, looking back upon it, feeling its reality, and stirred to the innermost depths of his spirit by its own peculiar influences. Just as Homer was the last of the rhapsodists, the last as well as the greatest minstrel of the heroic age in Greece, Scott feigned himself, and was indeed, as he has been called, 'the last and greatest of the Border minstrels.' The man and the circumstances met. A new interest in the old romances had been awakened by the mediæval revival, by the ballads of Bürger and other German poets, and by the publication of Percy's 'Reliques of Ancient Poetry' in 1765. 'I do not think,' said Wordsworth, 'that there is an able writer in verse of the present day who would not be proud to acknowledge his obligation to the *Reliques.*' The day on which Scott first opened that book he forgot dinner, he tells us, despite the sharp appetite of thirteen. The legends and tales of romance became his passion. He rapidly filled his mind with all that the poets and historians had written on these subjects, and dived deep into the forgotten antiquarian lore of charters and registers. But what was more important, he made, we may almost say *more Homerico,* raid after raid into Liddesdale, and from the lips of the country folk gathered the stories familiar to them from birth. These had for him a fascination and a truth no less keen or real than for the people to whom they were history and literature in one. 'Show me an old castle or a field of battle, and I was at home at once, filled it with its combatants in their proper costume, and overwhelmed my

hearers by the enthusiasm of my description.' Sir Phillip
Sidney declared that the old ballad of 'Percy and Douglas
roused him as did the sound of a trumpet; and upon the
youthful mind of Walter Scott, the effect of the stir and
ring of the like miniature epics was not dissimilar. From
1792 until 1798 he was constantly in the habit of making
ballad-forays into the heart of the country for direct oral
versions of well-known legends, and to obtain new and un-
known also. On one of these expeditions Scott discovered
the 'Ettrick Shepherd,' Hogg, now secure of remembrance
by the tenderness and quaint melody of the 'Queen's
Wake.' It was a notable find, not of a ballad, but of a
ballad-maker of truly original gifts. Two years after the
opening of the present century he published the result of
the raid in his book entitled 'Border Minstrelsy,' and in the
same year he began what was at first intended to be a ballad
of the same order—it was not his first experiment—but
which grew into a much greater work, 'The Lay of the
Last Minstrel.' In the opening of that poem we catch the
martial sounds which promised that the best battle-poetry
in the English tongue was about to be written.

> ' Nine and twenty knights of fame
> Hung their shields in Branksome Hall. . . .
> Ten of them were sheathed in steel,
> With belted sword and spur on heel ;
> They quitted not their harness bright,
> Neither by day nor yet by night ;
> They lay down to rest
> With corslet laced,
> Pillowed on buckler cold and hard ;
> They carved at the meal with gloves of steel,
> And they drank the red wine through the helmet barr'd.'

The ascendency of the classical school was at an end in

Germany as in England, and from Bürger and Goethe Scott had, before the publication of his ' Border Minstrelsy, made translations of poems in the same romantic spirit as his own native country's ballads. While Scott was thus engaged, Southey had been busy with 'Joan of Arc' and 'Thalaba.' Nothing is more evident than that the vitality of 'Marmion' or 'The Lay,' in contrast with the unreality, the tiresomeness, it must be confessed, despite the abundant poetic material they contain, of Southey's longer poems, is the direct result of the conditions which bring Scott into at least distant relationship with Homer. Scott's best poems have life; Southey's confessedly have not, although they are the work of a man of very marked poetic gifts. The life in the one case is due to the immediate personal contact of the author with the period to which his tales relate; the inertness and languor in the other are the inevitable result of any effort, however brilliant, to galvanise into life a dead body of material which has no relation to the times into which it is introduced for mere poetic purposes, and which was only known to the poet through the medium of books. In early life, Southey had devoted himself to the Titanic scheme of writing a poem upon each of the great mythologies of the world. It was a labour of the gods, and he braced himself nobly to the effort. In producing several poems, indisputably fine in conception and artistic in execution, he was successful. His figures are of heroic proportions, and their nobility enlists the reader's sympathy. The whole treatment of his themes is elevated and yet simple. Vitality alone is lacking, the fire of life to set all aglow, to set free the passions and thoughts, to call the statue from its pedestal to active existence amid the world of men. Neither as creator nor as maker did Southey possess the gifts of the first order which, as we have seen with Milton and Virgil, can dispense with an exciting body of fact in immediate mental proximity; and he was fated to deal with intractable, we may say with impossible, material. Yet when Southey has a good reader, whose imagination can supply what the poet himself was unable to do, he is a liberal giver. His friend Landor, a better artist, and happier in his subjects, but a poet in many respects akin to Southey—Landor, as also Scott and Taylor, were appreciative admirers. Byron spoke of 'Roderick' as 'the first poem of the time,' and for Coleridge there was a keen poetic pleasure in the 'pastoral charm and wild streaming lights of Thalaba.' These and other imaginative minds have appreciated Southey; but, more than any other English poet of equal name, he requires a good reader—a reader not merely receptive, but active. The high political excitement of the time does not occupy a large space in Southey's longer poems, although 'Joan of Arc,' his schoolboy epic, is Republican in sentiment. Nor was he a wanderer through the 'holy jungle of transcendental metaphysics,' in which Coleridge found and lost himself. Like Wordsworth, he could not go all lengths for liberty, believing that in so doing was involved defeat in victory; nor could he, what Shelley in his passionate enthusiasm went perilously near doing, join in—

'The braggart shout
For some blind glimpse of freedom.'

In eloquent and wise words he defended himself, when, speaking of certain of the friends of France, he said,—'They had turned their faces toward the east in the morning to worship the rising sun, and in the evening they were still looking eastward, obstinately affirming that still the sun was there. I, on the contrary, altered my position as the world went round.' Perhaps on one occasion only was his firm loyalty to the deep-rooted principles of his nature suffered to have full poetic expression—on the occasion of the 1814 negotiations with Buonaparte. On that occasion his verse was wrought to a correspondence with the white heat of righteous passion.

> ' Who counsels peace at this momentous hour,
>   When God hath given deliverance to the oppress'd,
>   And to the injured power?
>   Who counsels peace, when Vengeance like a flood
>   Rolls on, no longer now to be repress'd :
>   When innocent blood
>   From the four corners of the world cries out
>   For justice upon one accursed head :
>   When Freedom hath her holy banner spread
>   Over all nations, now in one just cause
>   United ; when with one sublime accord
>   Europe throws off the yoke abhorr'd,
>   And Loyalty, and Faith, and Ancient Laws
>   Follow the avenging sword !'

In the main, Southey's strength lay in the translation into equable verse, which neither crept nor soared, of habitual states of feeling in contact with inspiring but familiar thought. As a lyrist, he had no power of making his verses sing. There are no swift flashes of emotion, no keen joy nor piercing sorrow, such as shape the music of the true lyric poets, where the melody answers to the pulse of feeling. ' Poetry, he held,' says Professor Dowden, ' ought rather to elevate than affect — a Stoical doctrine transferred to art, which meant that his own poetry was derived more from admiration of great qualities than from sympathy with individual men or women.' Judged by his own canon,

Southey was a true poet. In the man, no less than in his poetry, all the heroic qualities meet. He sustained through life, as through the many volumes of verse and prose that were that life's high-hearted work, unswerving loyalty to his ideals.

In Aristotle's 'Poetics' it is laid down concerning the epic, 'that the story should be dramatically constructed like that of tragedy, and that it should have for its subject one entire and perfect action—having a beginning, a middle and an end; so that, forming like an animal a complete whole, it may afford its proper pleasure, widely differing from history in its construction ; because history necessarily treats, not of one action, but of one time, and of all the events that happened to one person or to many during that time—events the relation of which to each other is merely casual.' Scott can hardly be said to have written a poem fulfilling these conditions. Incident and scenery are more to us in his poems than the action as a whole. Had he respected the limitations of art, had he confined his genius, and given us one poem—say an epic of The Bruce—a task for which he was eminently fitted, we should perhaps have been richer than we are. If we were to speak accurately of Scott, we might call him a poet of epic genius, who never wrote save in fragments. His facility in narration, both in prose and verse, was so great that he ran on to undue lengths, never husbanding his powers. Passages of splendid fervour and force alternate with others careless, and even slovenly, in style. Rising at times to the true epic pitch, his verses fall at others to the level of doggerel ballad. He was quite incapable of careful revision, could not bring himself to re-handle a passage once thrown off, however hurriedly and carelessly. There is too much of his poetry, and he had not the patient art which, by repeated hours of toil, elevates or vitalises spaces destitute of dignity or life.

In 'The Lay of the Last Minstrel' and in 'Marmion,' we have Scott at his best, as he looks back upon the chivalric traditions of his native land. He was by nature soldier as much as poet, and loved the 'pluméd troop, the royal banner, the pride, pomp, and circumstance of glorious war.' In this he was like Homer, for he too was a soldier at heart, and

> 'Drank delight of battle with his peers
> Far on the ringing plains of windy Troy.'

Scott's mind was of no introspective type. A full, free, joyous life, in which the things of the body were as precious as the things of the mind, was what he loved. In this spirit of delight in war and heroic deeds, and in the spirit of simplicity which drew nothing from the musing melancholy of the age, but was concerned with the external world of action, rather than the internal of thought, he is Homeric. We find in him the closest approximation which English literature affords to the open-air atmosphere of the Greek epic poetry; but although in pictorial qualities, in their naturalness and unconscious spontaneity, in their firm but simple character-delineation, 'The Lay of the Last Minstrel,' 'Marmion,' 'The Lady of the Lake,' are of the same order of poetry as the 'Iliad' and the 'Odyssey,' in completeness of design and finish of execution, they fall manifestly behind the marvellous Greek. In 'The Lady of the Lake,' the scenery of the Scotch lakes is admirably sketched, as a background to a vividly picturesque description of Highland clan life; but it is not a poem through which the

Homeric ring and fire of battle sound and flash as in the former two; while in 'Rokeby,' 'The Lord of the Isles,' 'The Bridal of Triermain,' and the others, we have poems which were in reality tasks imposed upon the poet by reason of the success of his earlier work. These fall short in every great quality that earlier work displayed, and it displayed truly great qualities. No one who has felt the stir of Homeric fight, even in the names of the heroes, has breathed the air of battle, can fail to find the same quick pulsation and rising emotion accompany the lines of Scott,—

> ' Amid the scene of tumult, high
> They saw Lord Marmion's falcon fly :
> And stainless Tunstall's banner white,
> And Edmund Howard's lion bright,
> Still bear them bravely in the fight ;
>   Although against them come
> Of gallant Gordons many a one,
> And many a stubborn Badenoch-man,
> And many a rugged Border clan
>   With Huntly and with Home.'

From this passage to the end many of us will stand for it, that Marmion is a true epic fragment; it is a passage beside which there is no description of battle to be placed save Homer's.

> ' By this, though deep the evening fell,
> Still rose the battle's deadly swell,
> For still the Scots around their King,
> Unbroken, fought in desperate ring.
> Where's now their victor vanward wing,
>   Where Huntly and where Home?
> O, for a blast of that dread horn
> On Fontarabian echoes borne,
> That to King Charles did come,
>   When Rowland brave, and Olivier,

And every Paladin and peer,
On Roncesvalles died ! . . .
Front, flank and rear the squadrons sweep,
To break the Scottish circle deep,
   That fought around their King.
But yet, though thick the shafts as snow,
Though charging knights like whirlwinds go,
Though bill-men ply the ghastly blow,
   Unbroken was the ring ;
The stubborn spearmen still made good
Their dark impenetrable wood,
Each stepping where his comrade stood
   The instant that he fell.'

This description of the battle of Flodden—

   ' When shivered was fair Scotland's spear,
     And broken was her shield,'

is in its own way unapproached and unapproachable, and
whatever deductions may be made by the critics, with dif-
ficulty will some of us be persuaded that it will ever cease
to be read.   Scott's poetry, though it yielded the field
to Byron's versified tales, will never come to be classed
with them—the interest of the latter depends upon the
continual reappearance of the personality of the author,
it is not the broad human interest of 'The Lady of the
Lake' or 'Marmion.'   Byron's stories have already sunk
beneath the waters of oblivion, Scott's have survived despite
the total change in poetic fashions since his day.   They
may become obscured in periods of mental introspection,
but they will renew their youth with every revolt of the
natural man against the folly of neglecting one half of an
indivisible nature.   But Scott's greatness is not dependent
upon any one achievement.   He has an independent re-
putation in prose romance ; and were the Waverley Novels

and the longer narrative poems forgotten, the English-speaking peoples are not likely to prove such careless guardians of their lyric treasury as to lose poems which have the Shakesperian felicity of this, for example,—

> ' He is gone on the mountain,
>   He is lost to the forest
> Like a summer-dried fountain,
>   When our need was the sorest. . . .
> Fleet foot on the corrie,
>   Sage counsel in cumber,
> Red hand in the foray,
>   How sound is thy slumber ! '

Scott's lyrics are never expressive of the deeper or complex or spiritual emotion such as is rendered in Words-worth's or Tennyson's; Shelley's rapt intensity mirrors a world to which he was an entire stranger. But critics of the newer school are not always alive to his supremacy in his own lyrical sphere. A poem like the one just quoted, or that with its fiery lines, beginning,—

> ' Where shall the lover rest
> Whom the fates sever,'

are instinct with a full vitality of their own. They may seem of merely secondary excellence in comparison with poems which render into art subtle and composite spiritual experiences; but if so, the majority of Shakespere's lyrics, as those of Ben Jonson and of Milton, are also of secondary excellence. The bare simplicity of Scott's style misleads the reader who is accustomed to thread the tortuous mazes of the sonnets in 'The House of Life' or of 'The Sage Enamoured,' or any other of the poems of the later lyrists. But, as has been already more than once repeated, that bare simplicity is itself the mark of the highest art. It gives the impression of ease—a delusive impression, for

M

lucidity, though it may be the sign of the obvious and commonplace, is also the last and most signal triumph achieved by the consummate artist.

'Friends to precision of epithet will probably deny Scott's title to the name "great,"' says Carlyle. And again, 'The candid judge will in general require that a speaker in so extremely serious a universe as this of ours have something to speak about. In the heart of the speaker there ought to be some kind of gospel tidings, burning till it be uttered; otherwise it were better for him that he altogether held his peace. A gospel somewhat more decisive than this of Scott's.' The enthusiastic reformer, burning with apostolic zeal, is not altogether a trustworthy guide if he insist on measuring all things in heaven and earth with the line and plummet of his own creed. There are some of us, who are willing, even in our comparatively docile and spiritual moods, if we have any such, to give in exchange many recent volumes of gospel tidings for the fresh wild-wood music of a lyric by Shakespere or by Scott. He has 'written nothing which appeals to the immortal part of man,' it has been hastily, but not well said. It is not credible. The impulse of delight in beauty, in heroic action, in pure human affections, in nobleness, fortitude, gentleness, spring from the immortal part of man, else is there little immortal in him. To noble impulses and emotions, none the less real because universal and familiar, Scott ministers. To breathe his air is to strengthen the better side of ourselves, not the worser, just as to breathe pure air is to strengthen the physical condition of the body. To widen our human sympathies is to do us spiritual service.

Preference for the poetry of hysterical emotion or pessi

mistic threnes to a poem like 'Marmion' or like 'Rosabelle,' is of the same order as a preference of Shelley to Shakespere. If there be nothing in the poetry left by Scott that appeals to the immortal part of man, then must Chaucer, who 'fleets the time carelessly,' be removed from the roll of the masters, as also the Shakespere of the early comedies; for they teach us no gospel save the gospel of healthy delight in all pure and wholesome things, in all things that gladden the eye or quicken the pulse with elemental joys. Only the man in whose veins runs not human blood, but some thin spiritual or intellectual ichor, can deny Scott's right to noble place among the poets. It cannot be argued that he supplies nourishment for all moods of mind; neither is any other, save Shakespere, able to supply it. Who cares for Milton or Wordsworth when the pulses throng with the mere delight of living? How would Shelley sound, if read aloud, as Scott has been read, to soldiers in the midst of battle?* 'The rude man,' quotes Carlyle from some other writer, 'requires only to see something going on. The man of more refinement must be made to feel. The man of complete refinement must be made to reflect.' This is indisputable; but it does not at all militate against the poetry of Scott that it is enjoyed by some people who cannot enjoy, let us say Browning. There is, too, a class of people who enjoy Browning and fondly imagine that, in so doing, they are lovers of the finer aspects of poetry, when it may well be that they are merely students of psychology or metaphysics. Like most poets Scott only reached the rare, the memorable, the perfect at intervals; let us freely grant it, at long intervals. He might, had he been a less hasty workman, have reached it oftener, though that is doubtful. As it is

* Lockhart's *Life of Scott*, vol. iii. p. 327.

in ballad poetry he is incomparably first of English poets, and in a dozen of his best lyrics we have the intensity and simplicity, the unforgetable melody of song that cannot die. It is enough. Many a brightly shining poetic name is associated in our minds with but very few such immortal poems. Gray did no more, Goldsmith did no more, Burns did no more, nor Keats, nor Coleridge. The poetic reputation of Scott is with these, and, as Mr Swinburne would phrase it, 'he has his station for all time among the greater and the lesser stars.'

The characterisation in the poems is secondary to the incident and picturesque elements: it is sharper and clearer in the novels, though never subtle or deep-reaching. The refinements of soul-dissection or the therapeutics of mental disease were not branches of his art, and he rather shirked any contact with conditions that showed symptoms of abnormality, that were not in the ordinary way of life. When such conditions are introduced they are slightly treated and never analysed. The theological novel had not been discovered in Scott's time; had it been he would have shunned it as the plague. As Bagehot says in his admirable critique on the Waverley Novels, 'The desire to attain a belief, which has become one of the most familiar sentiments of heroes and heroines, would have seemed utterly incongruous to the plain sagacity of Scott, and also to his old-fashioned art. Creeds are *data* in his novels; people have different creeds, but each keeps his own.' Scott preferred the life of the outward world, where a choice had to be made, to the life of the inward. 'Life could not be endured,' he once said, 'were it seen in reality.' Scott was aware of, though he disliked to touch upon, the problem in its darker phases. He preferred to keep his eye on the

surface of things, and what an eye he had for the brave
display of splendid squadrons, the presence and princely
look of a hero, the beauty of face and grace of movement of
a girl, the colours of nature among his own 'honest grey
hills.' For the inner graces of the mind, for 'the mystery
that underlies all beauty,' he had not the same keen or appre-
ciative sense. He preferred the outward world, and he is a
poet of the outward world; in some respects, as for instance
in boldness of handling his subjects, like Byron, but superior
to him in 'hurried frankness of style.' 'Marmion,' we are
told, was partly composed on horseback, and the poem, as has
often been noticed, reproduces the rush and buoyant swing
of a striding steed. With Scott, as with Chaucer, we are up
with the sun and out in the morning air. The smoke and
dust of the city, with its ledgers and its bargains are behind
us, and our minds are carried at sight of ruined castle or
field of ancient fight to a time when men's lives were lived
on mountain side or within fortress walls, a time when bar-
gains were driven with the sword, and the commercial prin-
ciple was

> 'That they should take who have the power,
> And they should keep who can.'

Doubtless, the charm with which Scott invests these times
is a misleading charm. We know that, however delightful
they may now seem to us, these times were not as good as
our own much-abused and tiresome times. We are the
victims of a delusion, and we know it. We give ourselves to
it, because it is a pleasant delusion. We forget willingly that
cruelty and injustice overshadowed and rendered miserable
the lives of by far the greater number of the people; that,
whatever might be the pleasures of the life of a knight or of

a lady, and they were not unalloyed, the peasant and the common soldier were in no such happy case. But it is, after all, a delusion in which no poison lurks. To enjoy the life in imagination, or that side of it which is presented to us, which had its indisputably noble and picturesque aspects—this is surely the most harmless of innocent imaginings. But, to Carlyle, it is an ignoble lulling of ourselves to false though pleasant dreams. 'The reader sighed, "Oh, that I too had lived in those times, had never known these logic-cobwebs, this doubt, this sickliness; and been and felt myself alive among men alive!"' So far, the impeachment is not a heavy one; we may plead guilty to such occasional lapses from a wise and permanent preference for doubt and sickliness, which are realities and present, to heroisms and an heroic age which are fanciful and remote. But 'It was for the reader, not the El Dorado only, but a beatific land of Cockaigne and Paradise of Do-Nothings. The reader, what the vast majority of readers so long to do, was allowed to lie down at his ease and be ministered to. What the Turkish bath-keeper is said to aim at with his frictions and shampooing and fomentings, more or less effectually, that the patient, in total idleness, may have the delights of activity—was here to a considerable extent realised. The languid imagination fell back into its rest; an artist was here who could supply it with high-painted scenes, with sequences of stirring action, and whisper to it, "Be at ease, and let the tepid element be comfortable to thee."' It would have been a hazardous venture to speak in Carlyle's presence of art for art's sake. But direct didacticism is painfully ineffective in poetry. There is much discouragement in the fact that moral precept, more especially when obvious and unassailable, is abhorred by the Muses as a vacuum is abhorred by Nature; they have their own methods, but among the Nine there is no free use of the Pulpit. Consider a poem of Scott's which cannot by any dexterous management be made to yield a spiritual lesson—'The Gathering Song of Donald the Black.' Matthew Arnold spoke of 'The Lays of Ancient Rome' as 'pinchbeck ballads;' perhaps this and kindred pieces are 'pinchbeck ballads.' It may, at least, be safely said that the most skilful interpreter will find it difficult to extract from it any 'gospel-tidings.' Laying aside any claim for it as high poetry, it is a poem capable of giving a quickened sense of life, it affords pleasure. The pleasure afforded is not an immoral pleasure; and if innocent, are the sources of innocent pleasure so numerous that one can be spared? He is no lover of humanity who would not have them tenfold increased. Serious as life is, let us be on our guard lest we impoverish ourselves, let us go warily when we would purchase out abuses,—

'Nor deem that localised Romance
        Plays false with our affections;
Unsanctifies our tears—made sport
        For fanciful dejections;
Ah, no ! the visions of the past
        Sustain the heart in feeling
Life as she is—our changeful Life,
        With friends and kindred dealing.'

Carlyle himself was far from blind to the real worth of Scott. While he withheld from him the praise he rightly judged the highest—the praise that belongs to those who have lifted their fellows nearer the heaven of divine truth—he recognised the nobility of the man. 'Yet, on the other hand, the surliest critic must allow that Scott was a genuine man, which itself is a great matter.   No affectation, fantasticality or distortion dwelt in him; no shadow of cant Nay, withal, was he not a right brave and strong man, according to his kind?   What a load of toil, what a measure of felicity he quietly bore along with him : with what quiet strength he both worked on this earth and enjoyed in it; invincible to evil fortune and to good!   A most composed, invincible man; in difficulty and distress knowing no discouragement.   Samson - like, carrying off on his strong Samson shoulders the gates that would imprison him; in danger and menace, laughing at the whisper of fear.   And then, with such a sunny current of true humour and humanity, a free, joyful sympathy with so many things. . . . An eminently well-conditioned man—healthy in body, healthy in soul—we will call him one of the *healthiest* of men.   Neither is this a small matter; health is a great matter, both to the possessor of it and to others.'   Thus is Carlyle the prophet answered by Carlyle the man, in some respects the wiser individual.   Health is indeed a great matter, both to the possessor of it and to others! We are tempted to call it the greatest, the chiefest of matters.

'Scott became the historiographer royal of feudalism,' says Arnold, somewhat regretfully.   If a man is born capable above all other men of becoming a magnificent chronicler of the past, capable of becoming such an historiographer royal of feudalism as Scott was, why should we desire that his natural genius should be forcibly driven into other channels? A consummate master of the art of battle description might not prove a powerful street preacher, or shine a conspicuous figure before the footlights.   Scott's talent was a rare, an

extremely rare one; it was worthily employed. Our edu-
cators tell us that the cardinal principle of progress is to
discover and direct the natural bent of the individual mind,
that thus and only thus we become gainers, that in the
effort to thwart Nature men are rarely successful. Like
Landor and Keats, Scott was not a son of his own genera-
tion; he was born, a happy fortune for us, a century too
late. From the new armoury of ideas that came with the
'drums and tramplings' of the opening century, he chose
not a single weapon. We may regret that he did not go
deep enough into human life to give us any ideal hero like
the 'Happy Warrior' of Wordsworth; but his work could
not have been done by another. His range was on the
whole wider than that of any writer since Shakespere, and
even the poetic headings of the chapters of his novels are
sufficient to prove the width of that range. Take this in a
style not characteristic of him; does it not approach the
manner of Shakespere himself?—

> ' The storm increases; 'tis no sunny shower,
> Foster'd in the moist breast of March or April,
> Or such as parchèd summer cools his lips with.
> Heaven's windows are flung wide; the inmost deeps
> Call, in hoarse greeting, one upon another;
> On comes the flood in all its foaming horrors,
> And where's the dike shall stop it ?'

Scott's passion for humanity was such as belongs to the
great poets. Nature, especially in her sterner and more
solitary Border country aspects, he loved with a very deep
and true affection. 'If I did not see the heather at least
once a year, I think I should die,' he said. His descriptions
are unmarked by any meditative insight, by any 'sense of
something far more deeply interfused,' whose dwelling-place

Nature is—we do not expect it—but they call up a very vivid impression of the scene or the object. Through Scott many who have thought themselves destitute of the poetic sense have made their way into the realm of gold. He was successful in calling the attention of the civilised world to the beauties and the history of his native country. His magic wand called into life its buried heroes and forgotten traditions, and without him the advancing tide of civilisation would have obliterated every ancient land-mark, and the heroic age of Scotland would have been as completely sunk and hidden beneath its waves as the round towers of Ireland that lie beneath the waters of its greatest lake.

In width of human sympathy Scott is with Shakespeare. With what better word can we take leave of him ? He has created for us, and creation must rank before philosophising or the literary arts of polishing and refining ; creation counts for more. Tory as Scott consistently was, he did no wrong to political foes in any of his writings. That large-souled, humorous, joyous man touched life at a vast number of points. He did not touch it at the point we are accustomed, perhaps truly, to regard as the most vital of all, the point at which its circle meets the greater circle whose centre is the source of all being, and whose circumference is not coincident with any physical horizon. This was his limitation, partly conscious and deliberate, but it was not such a limitation as enfeebles though it may restrict art. Nor was it sufficient, in the minds of many as good friends to precision of epithet as Carlyle, to reverse the testimony of his contemporaries to his greatness. Tennyson spoke the sentiment of the English - speaking peoples when in his last days he wrote,—

' Oh, great and gallant Scott,
True gentleman, heart, blood and bone ;
    I would it had been my lot,
To have seen thee, and, heard thee and known.'

Southey and Scott were not the greatest poets of their age, but they were its best as well as its greatest men. The laurel is not only the meed of mighty conquerors and poets sage, it is earned by all signal service in the estates of the universal human realm.

CHAPTER IX

THE PARTING OF THE WAYS

* Tennyson—Arnold—Browning

BEFORE the *Sturm und Drang* of the first quarter of the present century had perceptibly abated, while England was engaged in the momentous struggle for her own liberty and that of Europe, while the new revolutionary and spiritual ideas were still powerfully exciting motors to action and thought, literature responded to the high-beating pulse of the time. It was passion - full, sometimes fevered, at all times in unison with the thrill and stir of a nation's hour of heightened vitality. Poetry was its natural voice; but with the succeeding calm, with the quieter, steadier pulse of the body politic and social, came the era of prose, representative of mental equanimity; of the novel, affording artificial stimulus to compensate for the loss of exciting causes in the real world; of æsthetic and scientific enquiry, only possible to a people who have leisure, who are unoccupied with pressing questions of foreign policy affecting their national existence; of studied art, less spontaneous, less the result of the direct inspiration of an exciting period, but more

* The reader is referred to the chapter entitled ' Neo-Classicism,' and to Professor Dowden's suggestive essay on Tennyson and Browning, in his *Studies in Literature*.

perfect as regards form ; in short, an era dominated by the critical rather than by the productive spirit. Out of the philosophic revival grew the mastering modern principles of scientific investigation ; out of the ideas brought into prominence by the Revolution came the mastering modern principles at work, modifying social and political conditions, towards the levelling up and the levelling down aimed at by our Socialist reformers. Without attempting to map out the numerous conflicting influences in our present world of English thought, we may name these as chief. A close observer of the history of the century will note that, while the democratic spirit and the scientific spirit have gathered strength with the years, have justified themselves with time, there has been no corresponding gain to spiritual ideals, to the strengthening and deepening of a faith in the unseen world, or to the idea of its virtual union with this. There has been no corresponding justification of the transcendental philosophy, of the impulse towards the creed that holds by an indwelling spiritual presence, that brought the divine into close communion with the human mind, that read in Nature's beauties and sublimities the signs manual of an everlasting hyper-physical power. The increase of strength to the democratic and scientific principles has worked against spiritualism, against the transcendental movement so potent in the early years of the century ; for, as has often been observed, all forms of supernaturalism fare ill in an era of democracy, or during the reign of a scientific spirit. Democracy and science are hostile to things that are not very near, that cannot be taken as it were into the hand, to things that they do not understand. Democracy rarely lifts its eyes above or beyond material ideals, above the gratified or delighted contemplation of bodily comforts, of high wages,

short hours and cheap luxuries. Even in 'Chants for
Socialists' it will be vain to look for any conception beyond
such a very excellent one as this :—

> ' The little house on the hill,
> The streams and the woodland beauty, and the happy fields we till ;
> And the artist's hand of wonder, and the marvellous fiddle bow,
> And the banded choirs of music, all those that do and know.'

In a word, a Greek, not a Christian ideal ; for there is not a
hint of a life other than this, which we had fondly hoped
was but a stage on an infinite journey.   Scientific investi-
gation, too, is unfriendly to any desire of the soul for other
and better worlds.   Admirably adapted for attainment of
truth, in respect of such things as may be examined under
the microscope, or thoroughly probed and laid bare under
the scalpel, its very incapacity to go further is the most con-
clusive of arguments that there is no further to go.   The
microscope has not yet revealed soul, the dissecting knife
has never yet grated against mind, and, for the same reason,
God has not, up to the present, been brought into the as-
tronomers' field of vision by the best telescopes.   The exist-
ence of God and the soul is, therefore, wisely discredited ;
had they any real objective existence, outside the dreaming
imagination of mankind, they could not have escaped the
trained eye of the keen physicists.   The allegiance of the
peoples is transferred to the things that may be seen and
handled.   Democracy has been justified, scientific methods
have been triumphantly justified.   Traditional religious be-
lief has at least historical evidence for its support, and can
never lose its hold upon a certain type of mind, but the
transcendental philosophy has not been justified by experi-
ment.   It matters not that its creed is unverifiable by ex-

periment. In a scientific age, creeds that are unverifiable
by experiment, that cannot commit their tenets to the testing
instruments and acids of the Savant, are in the same position
as beliefs that are negatived by experiment; such creeds are
no longer credited or credible. In an age of progress, more-
over, creeds that offer nothing appetisingly new are neglected
in the search after what may feed the universal hunger for the
hitherto unknown or unobserved. There has been progress
in our knowledge of Nature, and in our command over her;
but there has been no corresponding increase of spiritual
knowledge. The spectroscope therefore lords it over the
wearyingly familiar facts about the soul and the moral sense.
Material advance is of the race, it does not greatly profit
the spirit of man; but it is not the race but the individua
that grows in grace. No observer can fail to note the re-
turn, in English thought—the thought of a people not long
to be diverted from what is called the practical view of
things—to the mental standpoints of the eighteenth century.
Attention is once more withdrawn from the consideration of
subjects bordering upon the insoluble, from delight in a full
free naturalism, its passions and enthusiasms, to subjects
near at hand, an investigation of which may be useful, and
will, at all events, certainly lead to definite results. While
the paramount nineteenth-century ideals are nobler and
more comprehensive than those of the eighteenth century,
they have not lost their old materialistic character. The
literature dominated by the scientific and democratic spirit
has for its aim the gradual amelioration of existing evils, the
improvement of the conditions of life, leading to a far off
but attainable commonwealth of healthy and prosperous
persons. The classic ideal, rather than the Christian, is
apparent throughout all that literature. The state bulks

more largely than the individual, whose spiritual or moral condition, except in so far as it tends to the greatest happiness of the greatest number, is of small account. The consummation will be reached in the latter days, many souls must be sacrificed ere it come, as millions have already been sacrificed, 'to the insatiable Moloch of the evolution principle;' and other goal than that of the future happiness of the race is not contemplated by it. With this school of thought we are once more in an eighteenth century of widened intellectual and moral horizon, but as impatient as ever of ideas not definitely seized, of all forms of mysticism, of belief in things not seen ; a school of thought represented by a literature which idolises the capitalised experience of the race; utilitarian and limited, but unquestionably beneficial in raising the general standard of intelligence to a respectable mediocrity. Accompanying the faith in ideas useful, clear and tangible, we have a revival of classic art, of precision in substance and highly-wrought perfection in form. Its highest reach is in the poetry of Tennyson. Compare his vision of life, broader, deeper and richer as it undoubtedly is, with that of the earlier classical school. The ethical note rings clear and distinct in it ; the ethics, as before, are the ethics of obedience to law, and disorder and confusion are the worst of evils. In this conception of the world, the place of the Architect, Who originally, as Pope conceived it, 'framed the wondrous whole,' but had since kept at a distance from His creation, is taken by a moral Lawgiver ; and it is instructive to note that Tennyson leaned towards the theory of a Demiurge,* as an explanation of the facts of the world.

* '*Nineteenth Century*,' January 1893.—'Aspects of Tennyson,' by the Editor.

The floodtide of Transcendentalism was not long at the full in England. The cry was soon raised, that once more we were engaged with shadows; and when the scientific methods were crowned with numerous successes, belief on other than scientific grounds became for many impossible. The Stoic spirit of acceptance with sad content of whatever relative truth may be gained, has once more been widely preached. One aspect of that Stoic acceptance was exhibited in the poetry of Matthew Arnold—where sorrow for a beautiful but lost faith, a wistful regret, mingles with a contempt for the belauded benefits of a material civilisation; and with the forced calm, the high moral purpose, such as supported Marcus Aurelius in the imperial purple and Epictetus in the garb of a slave. But it is with Tennyson that the cycle may properly be said to close. The Tennyson of the early poems—of 'Locksley Hall' and 'The Princess'—was the direct spokesman of the times. The successes of Science, the gains to humanity since it had embraced the new and wise spirit of progress, are celebrated with due fervour,—

' The fairy tales of Science and the long results of time.'

But the early liberalism of youth could not go all lengths, and the natural conservatism of the poet reasserted itself. Science, beyond a certain point, democratic principles, or measures heralded by revolution or pushed heatedly, without regard to aristocratic vested interests, became obnoxious. Tennyson's imagination ran in English rather than in disinterested world-wide grooves. There was a limit to his enthusiasm; he throws off his allegiance to Science when she presumes too far—

N

> ' Not only cunning casts in clay
> Let Science prove we are, and then
> What matter Science unto men,
> At least to me ?   I would not stay.'

His love of freedom is temperate ; like Shakespere, he cannot put trust in the shouts of the mob,—

> ' A love of freedom, rarely felt,
> Of freedom in her regal seat
> Of England ; not the schoolboy heat,
> The blind hysterics of the Celt.'

With the scientific and the democratic movements, Tennyson went joyfully a little way, hymning their praises ; but he did not give himself unreservedly to one or to the other. It is impossible for any great poet to rest wholly satisfied with the things of the body, with mechanical advantages and an increase of earthly happiness. Holding firmly by tradition with one hand, he could only give the other to the pioneers of the progressive schools of thought ; and when it came to be necessary to relinquish one or other, he made choice of the older friend, tradition, the long witness of mankind to facts of a spiritual world of which they had no scientific evidence, but from which they have never been able, and never will be able, to part. To these noble traditions he remained loyal, and to them, as interpreted by the Broad Church party ; but without, even in ' In Memoriam,' falling back upon the support offered by Transcendentalism. Nevertheless, Tennyson is not unreservedly an exponent or a representative of Christian, but of classic art. He held by Plato, perhaps, as firmly as he held by Christian revelation. Arnold was the representative of the later culture which held by Plato more firmly than by Christian revelation ; held by his ethics, at least, and those

of Marcus Aurelius and of Epictetus and of Spinoza.
Browning alone of the poets of the latter half of the
century remained unshaken by the revelations of Science,
disdainful of the mere mechanical progress of the race—
remained true to Christianity, to the new readings of it
given by Transcendentalism, to the sacredness of individual
life, to the principle that the realisation of an ideal like
that of the 'Parliament of man, the federation of the world,'
is as small dust in the balance, compared with the awaken-
ing to life of a single soul; and he is therefore the only
representative of Christian art in an era of classical revival.

Tennyson's classic spirit as opposed to any spirit of
mysticism comes out in this, that just as the Greek artists,
although they recognised the impossibility of satisfaction
with the attainment of finite ideals, but out of the obscure
longings of the heart for some infinitely enduring affection,
for some eternal rock unmoved amid the waves of change—
out of these, or out of the unutterable desires that from their
secret sources well up in every human breast, desires for in-
finite love, passions for infinite perfection, could forge no
weapon to storm a higher height, and for the purposes of art
remained deliberately at a point whence all that was seen
was seen sharply and fully, so the Tennyson of the early
poems admitted to his verse only those conceptions that
are capable of complete realisation, and may be adequately
expressed. Life, as it is conditioned by space and time
and things seen, was accepted by him without suggestion
as to its sufficiency or insufficiency to satisfy the whole
nature of man, mind and heart and soul. As already
noticed, the first principles of classic art are involved in
this — to treat only of the known: and while Tennyson
insists on a future life as necessary to make this life in-

telligible, to save us from permanent intellectual confusion, that other life is rarely brought into any close relationship with the present.   It is a necessary hypothesis, but one which does not to any degree affect the present life.   Meanwhile an ideal of this world will be helpful.   Let it consist in the progress glorified by the Evolutionist, and an eventual Millennium; let it here and now, in this life, consist in a determination to acquire an universal dominion over the powers of Nature, that vast reservoir of forces that may be fettered and worked, the giant slaves of man who has hit upon the great open secret that knowledge is power; let us band together that we may have the very best bread that can be made from wheat, both for ourselves and for our descendants.   Such is the definite ideal which must encourage

     ' Men our brothers, men the workers, ever reaping something new,
       That which they have done but earnest of the things they yet
         shall do.'

In the contemplation of such an ideal Tennyson rested he was inspired and aroused by these splendid glimpses as neither Arnold nor Browning could have been.   For him it would be sufficient happiness to rise—not to return from some other sphere of activity—but to *rise* once in every hundred years

       ' And learn the world and sleep again, . . .
        And wake on science grown to more
        On secrets of the brain, the stars
        As wild as aught of fairy lore ;
        And all that else the years will show.'

Compare with this the world-weariness of the poet of the later culture.   To him it seems that for one who has served

men nobly and acceptance found, nothing is to be preferred
to rest, lasting rest.

> ' Why should he pray to range
> Down the long age of truth that ripens slow,
> And vex his heart with all the baffling change
> And all the tedious tossing to and fro ? '

Compare with it also the feeling of insufficiency in things
seen, however gratifying to ordinary human senses, dis-
played all through the poetry of Browning. His is indeed
an unwearied delight in beauty, in all that the world holds
fair and good and great, in all that Nature offers of colour
or form ; but it is a delight merely in passing, a delight
on the way to grander, more subtile, more complex delight
in the ardours and loves and enthusiasms of the soul which
are the instruments of its ever-renewed awakening, of its
expansion and infinite growth, a feeling that may be com-
pressed into one line—

> ' How inexhaustibly the spirit grows ! '

Tennyson, closing an epoch, gathers to himself something
from all the movements of thought that have preceded
him. He is the poet of generalisations, who sums up the
intellectual and moral gains of humanity, all that it has
learned through experience, and is the supreme representa-
tive in English of the poetry of culture, the poetry that
is a 'criticism of life.' We see in him what may be
accomplished by pure art joined to wide knowledge ; his
poetry is in this no less classic in form than in spirit, that
he was even a more careful student of his expression than
of his substance.

We may trace yet another classic tendency in Tennyson's
sustained interest in the history of the race rather than in

that of the individual soul, in his anticipation of a definite end of all men's labours, of the 'toil co-operant to an end.' It is not so much, even in the later poems of wider grasp and deeper meaning, a man's duty to himself, to his higher spiritual nature, as his duty to the state, to his fellow men, that occupies his attention. Looking back, as we have seen, upon the history of the world, he feels and expresses a natural joy in all that man has done; looking forward, he contemplates with hope what the race may yet in the future do; but he has concerned himself little with the marvellous inner world, the complexities of man's emotional and spiritual nature, of the soul battling with itself, rising by repeated and continued effort, or ruined by a failure of will or contentment with the attainment of some mean or sordid ambition. Tennyson, concerned with large social and political results, takes no note of the crises in the development or deterioration of the individual. The suffering and failure which each man undergoes are not conceived as throughout educative, or brought into place as a necessary step towards the perfect life. He is indeed conscious that

' Men may rise on stepping-stones
Of their dead selves to higher things; '

but he nowhere encourages noble ventures that may lead to earthly failure, but which may also lead to magnificent recompense in heart and spirit. This life of restraint, of 'self-reverence, self-knowledge, self-control,' is the ideal of Stoicism, and the ideal of the Greek philosophers who were not Stoics, like Plato or Epicurus; it fears failure in obedience, confusions and disorders; the Christian life, as interpreted by Browning, fears ignoble satisfactions, counsels a noble discontent, a splendid restlessness, a multiplication, strengthening and development in every direction of the spiritual part of us. The future of the race upon earth does not greatly trouble Browning, he does not care to see to the end, nor is he dazzled by bright visions of a positivist paradise. His imagination wanders through the infinite deeps of the individual soul, his poetry is sacred to individual aspirations prophetic of the spirit's destiny.

The minor poets are of the school of Tennyson, of the subjective school or of the classic school; Browning, the dramatist, the student of the human soul, has but few followers. The narrowing in of the poetic horizon, the dearth of inspiring motives have driven the poets to a fashioning of delicate filigree work, of dainty devices, sometimes in revived, always in quaint and fanciful forms. Like Mr William Morris, the majority feel themselves to be 'idle singers of an empty day.' While Tennyson and the poets of culture bring the era to a close, Browning's subjects and methods, so unique, so independent of contemporary fashions, seem prophetic of a new. If Tennyson sums up the gains to the higher civilisation, Browning must be regarded as one of the renewers of the world's thought, a master builder who quarries his own marbles—somewhat roughly, it must be confessed—fashions and grinds his own tools, and builds on his own plans. He left it to others to preach the virtue of balanced liberalism, of practical, high-minded common sense, of loyalty to all noble memories of his native land, allegiance to a heritage of splendid traditions, sober freedom, equal laws, chivalrous manners; and pushed out into that unexplored and inexhaustible world of man's hidden and eternal nature, all earnest, bold and overbold, as a man and a poet must be who attempts something widely different from a finished representation of the beautiful and finite — a search into the obscure, deeply - hidden, yet omnipresent and everywhere recognisable infinite, whether in man or Nature, a quest which is none other than a quest for 'God's first creature, which is Light.'

APPENDIX.

——o——

CHRONOLOGICAL TABLE OF ENGLISH LITERATURE
From 1770 to 1870.

1770.—Chatterton died. Wordsworth born. Letters of Junius. Burke—
Thoughts on the Present Discontents. (Gœthe's 'Götz von
Berlichingen.' Bürger's ' Lenore.')

1771.—Gray died, Scott born.

1772.—Coleridge born. (Lessing's 'Emilia Galotti.')

1773.—Ferguson's poems. Goldsmith's 'She Stoops to Conquer.'

1774. –Southey born. (Gœthe's ' Werther.') Goldsmith died. Berkeley's
' Siris.'

1775.—Savage Landor born. Lamb born.

1776.—Cowper begins to write.

1777.—Campbell born. Henry Hallam born.

1778. –Hazlitt born. Cowper's Olney Hymns composed.

1779.—Moore born. Garrick died. Sheridan's ' Critic.'

1780.—Johnson's ' Lives of the Poets.'

1781.—Crabbe's ' Library.' Darwin's ' Botanic Garden.' (Kant's ' Kritik
der Reinen Vernunft.')

1782.—Cowper's first volume of poems.

1783.—Crabbe's 'Village.' Blake's ' Poetical Sketches.'

1784.—Johnson died. Leigh Hunt born.

1785. –De Quincey born. Peacock born. Cowper's 'Task.'

1786.—Burns' first poems.

1787.—Burns' poems ; second issue.

1788.—Byron born. The *Times* newspaper.

1789.—Blake's ' Songs of Innocence.' Bowles' ' Sonnets.' Darwin's ' Loves
of the Plants.'

1790.—(French Revolution.)

1791.—Boswell's ' Life of Johnson.'

1792.—Shelley born. Paine's ' Age of Reason.'

1793.—Wordsworth's ' Descriptive Sketches.' Godwin's ' Political Justice.'
Roger's ' Pleasures of Memory.'

201

1794.—Southey's 'Wat Tyler.' Blake's 'Songs of Experience.'

1795.—Keats born. Carlyle born. Landor's first poems.

1796.—Burns died. Hartley Coleridge born. Burke's 'Letters on a Regicide Peace.'

1797.—Southey's poems. Coleridge's *Annus Mirabilis.*'

1798.—Lyrical Ballads by Wordsworth and Coleridge. Landor's 'Gebir.'

1799.—Hood born. Campbell's 'Pleasures of Hope.'

1800.—Cowper died. Macaulay born. Coleridge's 'Translation of Schiller.'

1801.—Southey's 'Thalaba.' Moore's 'Anacreon.' Newman born.

1802.—Scott's 'Border Minstrelsy.' *Edinburgh Review.* (Victor Hugo born.)

1803.—Mrs Heman's first poems.

1804.—(Bonaparte, Emperor. Kant died.)

1805.—Scott's 'Lay of the Last Minstrel.' Southey's 'Madoc.'

1806.—Coleridge's 'Christabel.' Peacock's 'Palmyra.' (Gœthe's 'Faust.')

1807.—Byron's 'Hours of Idleness.' Moore's 'Irish Melodies.' Crabbe's 'Parish Register.'

1808.—Scott's 'Marmion.' *Quarterly Review* established.

1809.—Alfred Tennyson born. E. B. Browning born. Charles Darwin born.

1810.—Crabbe's 'Borough.' Southey's 'Curse of Kehama.' Scott's 'Lady of the Lake.'

1811.—Thackeray born. Shelley's 'Necessity of Atheism.' J. Austen's 'Sense and Sensibility.'

1812.—Dickens born. Browning born. Byron's 'Childe Harold,' 1 and 2 cantos.

1813.—Shelley's 'Queen Mab.' Scott's 'Rokeby.' Hogg's 'Queen's Wake.'

1814.—Scott's 'Waverley.' Wordsworth's 'Excursion.' Southey's 'Roderick.' Byron's 'Corsair and Lara.' Cary's 'Translation of Dante.'

1815. Scott's 'Lord of the Isles' and 'Guy Mannering.' Byron's 'Hebrew Melodies.'

1816.—Byron left England. 'Childe Harold,' 3 canto, and 'Prisoner of Chillon.' Shelley's 'Alastor.'

1817.—Keats' first poems. Moore's 'Lalla Rookh.' Byron's 'Manfred.'

1818.—Keats' 'Endymion.' Shelley's 'Revolt of Islam.'

1819.—John Ruskin born. Charles Kingsley born. George Eliot born. Byron's 'Don Juan.' Crabbe's 'Tales of the Hall.'

1820.—Shelley's 'Prometheus.' and 'Cenci.' (Accession of George IV.)

1821.—Keats died. Shelley's 'Adonais.' De Quincey's 'Confessions.' Southey's 'Vision of Judgment.'

1822.--Shelley died. Matthew Arnold born.

1823.—Lamb's 'Essays of Elia.' Elliott's poems. Moore's 'Loves of the Angels.'

1824, –Byron died. Landor's 'Imaginary Conversations.'

1825.—Coleridge's 'Aids to Reflection.' T. Huxley born.

1826.—Carlyle's 'Life of Schiller.'

1827.—Blake died. 'Poems by Two Brothers.' Keble's 'Christian Year.'

1828.—D. G. Rossetti born. G. Meredith born. *Athenæum* and *Spectator* established.

1829.—Milman's 'History of the Jews.' Mill's 'Analysis of the Human Mind.'

1830.—Tennyson's first poems. Hazlitt died. (Accession of William IV.)

1831.—Landor's 'Count Julian.' Lytton's 'Eugene Aram.' Poe's 'Raven.'

1832.—Scott died. (Gœthe died.) Crabbe died. Leigh Hunt's Poetical Works.

1833.—Coleridge died. Charles Lamb died. Carlyle's 'Sartor Resartus.'

1834.--A. H. Hallam died. W. Morris born. 'Tracts for the Times.'

1835.–Hogg died. Browning's 'Paracelsus.' Alfred Austin born.

1836.—Dickens' 'Pickwick.' Landor's 'Pericles and Aspasia.'

1837.—Browning's 'Strafford.' A. C. Swinburne born. (Accession of Victoria.) Carlyle's 'French Revolution.'

1838.—Lecky born. Mrs Browning's 'Seraphim,' and other poems. Carlyle's 'Sartor Resartus.' Dickens' 'Nicholas Nickleby.'

1839.—Praed died. Carlyle's 'Chartism.'

1840.—Browning's 'Sordello.' Lever's 'Charles O'Malley.'

1841.—Browning's 'Bells and Pomegranates, 'Pippa Passes.' Carlyle's 'Heroes and Hero Worship.'

1842.—Browning's 'Dramatic Lyrics.' Macaulay's 'Lays of Ancient Rome.'

1843.—Southey died. Wordsworth became Poet Laureate. Macaulay's 'Lays of Ancient Rome.' Carlyle's 'Past and Present.' Ruskin's 'Modern Painters.'

1844.—Campbell died.

1845.—Hogg died. Lewes' 'History of Philosophy.'

1846.—Hookham Frere died. Carlyle's 'Oliver Cromwell.' Poems by C. E. and A. Brontë.

1847.—Landor's 'Hellenics.' Longfellow's 'Evangeline.' Thackeray's 'Vanity Fair.' L. Hunt's 'Honey from Mt. Hybla.' Tennyson's 'Princess.'

1848.—Clough's first poems. Lytton's 'Caxtons.' Mill's 'Political Economy.'

1849.—Matthew Arnold's first poems. Dickens' 'David Copperfield. Ruskin's 'Seven Lamps of Architecture.'

1850.—Wordsworth died. Bowles died. Tennyson's 'In Memoriam.'.

1851.—Mrs Browning's 'Casa Guidi Windows.' Carlyle's 'Life of Sterling.'

1852.—Moore died. Thackeray's 'Esmond.' Ruskin's 'Stones of Venice.'

1853.—Landor's 'Last Fruit off an Old Tree.'

1854.—Thackeray's 'Four Georges.' Newman's 'Idea of a University.'

1855.—Rogers died. Tennyson's 'Maud.' Kingsley's 'Westward Ho!'

1856.—Mrs Browning's 'Aurora Leigh.'

1857.—Matthew Arnold, Professor of Poetry at Oxford. (Béranger died. Comte died.)

1858.—Morris' 'Defence of Guenevere.' Longfellow's 'Miles Standish.'

1859.—De Quincey died. Macaulay died. Leigh Hunt died. Darwin's 'Origin of Species.' George Eliot's 'Adam Bede.'

1860.—George Eliot's 'Mill on the Floss.' Emerson's 'Conduct of Life.' Tyndall's 'Glaciers of the Alps.'

1861.—Mrs Browning died. A. H. Clough died. Mill's 'Representative Government.'

1862.—Spencer's 'First Principles.'

1863.—Thackeray died. George Eliot's 'Romola.'

1864.—Landor died. Tennyson's 'Enoch Arden.' Browning's 'Dramatis Personæ.' Swinburne's 'Atalanta in Calydon.'

1865.—William Morris' 'Life and Death of Jason.' Lecky's 'History of Rationalism.'

1866.—Swinburne's Poems and Ballads. George Eliot's 'Felix Holt.'

1867.—Carlyle's 'Shooting Niagara—and After?' (Renan's 'St Paul.')

1868.—Browning's 'Ring and the Book.'

1869.—Morris' 'Earthly Paradise.' (Sainte-Beuve died. Hartmann's 'Philosophy of the Unconscious.')

1870.—D. G. Rossetti's Poems. Newman's 'Grammar of Assent.' Arnold's 'St Paul and Protestantism.' Huxley's 'Lay Sermons.'

COLSTON AND COMPANY, PRINTERS, EDINBURGH.

O